CHARLES F. KEMP is currently Distinguished Professor of Pastoral Care at Brite Divinity School, Texas Christian University. He formerly was pastor for churches in New York, Iowa, and Nebraska.

Dr. Kemp earned A.B. and M.A. degrees at Drake University, a B.D. degree at Colgate-Rochester Divinity School, and a Ph.D. at the University of Nebraska. He also received an honorary D.D. degree from Drake University in 1963.

Dr. Kemp is a very prolific author. Among his books are *Life-Situation Preaching, The Pastor and Vocational Counseling, Preparing for the Ministry, The Church: The Gifted and the Retarded Child, The Pastor and Community Resources,* and *Pastoral Preaching.* He contributes a regular column to *The Christian* and has had articles published in several other religious magazines.

The author has been a frequent speaker during Religion-in-Life Week on college and university campuses and has also spoken often at ministers' institutes.

THE
Preaching Pastor

THE
Preaching Pastor

❧ ❧ ❧

BY CHARLES F. KEMP

THE BETHANY PRESS • ST. LOUIS, MISSOURI

Contents

Contents

Introduction

For more than nineteen hundred years the Christian faith has been perpetuated and lives have been changed by the power of preaching. Some of these changes have been sudden, dramatic, cataclysmic. Christian history is replete with examples of men whose lives have been transformed by what the Apostle Paul called "the folly of what we preach." Wilfred Grenfell drifted into a meeting where Dwight L. Moody was preaching, more because of curiosity than devotion, and his life was changed. John R. Mott attended a meeting on the Cornell campus where a visitor from England was preaching, and young Mott was so challenged that he made that night what he called a "life investment decision." A newspaper reporter, attracted by a crowd waiting to get into Riverside Church to hear Harry Emerson Fosdick preach, went in himself, primarily out of curiosity, and found that Fosdick spoke to his condition and turned him from despair to hope.

These illustrations could be multiplied indefinitely. We would not for a minute discount their validity or their value. In all honesty and fairness, however, we recognize that this does not often happen in the average church or to a very large percentage of people who attend Protestant worship services. This does not mean things do not happen. Change does take place, but, in the main, it is slow and gradual.

This is very similar to what happens in counseling. A person seeks out a counselor because he is nervous or anxious; he feels guilty or inadequate. As the two work together, the troubled person gradually gains new insights, takes new steps toward maturity, becomes more understanding and more confident. But it is slow. At times it seems that nothing at all is taking place, but as long as he continues in the process, things do occur.

Preaching is much like counseling in this respect. If the parishioner gains new insights now and then, makes a new resolve, gains the courage to try again, or receives assurance of divine resources, change is taking place. It may be small—almost imperceptible at times—but it is nonetheless real.

The vast majority of people who attend church need to experience such changes. They are professing Christians and do many good things, but they also fall far short of their desires and their possibilities. They know what's right, but they need the guidance, the assurance, and the inspiration to keep them moving in that direction. They need to move from doubt to faith, from anxiety to peace, from hostility to love, from self-centeredness to self-forgetfulness.

It is the conviction expressed in this volume that preaching can be a great help in this process. As a result, the sermons have been selected because we feel they fulfill this function. Preaching is closely related to counseling; one really supplements the other. For this reason, in the four introductory chapters and in the introductions to the various sections we have stressed the close relationship between preaching and pastoral care.

The sermons have been selected from the vast range of sermonic literature, both past and present, that is available. We have selected eight areas in which people need growth. Each area is introduced by a statement emphasizing its importance. Sermons have been chosen that illustrate how this area of need has been met and can be met through preaching. Included in each area are two sermons, one that was preached a generation or so ago (we have much to learn from these men who proved their ability to meet human needs) and one from contemporary preaching (it is helpful to know what other men are doing). We hope that these examples of preaching will be helpful to men who are serving as preachers and pastors today.

❧ ❧ ❧

We wish to express our appreciation to all the authors of the sermons and the publishers who have so generously granted permission for their material to be included. We have made every effort to trace the source of all quotations and to give due credit to all authors and publishers. If there have been any omissions because it was impossible to locate the original source, we offer our sincere apologies.

PART I

The Preaching Pastor

❧

Preaching to Human Needs

❧

Preaching for Continued Growth

❧

That They Might Become Saints

Chapter 1

The Preaching Pastor

The great preachers have usually been faithful pastors. The great pastors have very often been effective preachers.

The two terms that have been used most frequently throughout history to describe the minister have been the words "prophet" and "shepherd." They have quite different connotations. One term brings to mind the work of the preacher, the other the work of the pastor.

The literature that has to do with the work of the ministry has usually emphasized one or the other. The literature on homiletics has stressed the minister's prophetic role; the literature on pastoral theology or, more recently, pastoral counseling and pastoral care has stressed the shepherding role.

Some feel there is a radical difference between the two roles, that one cannot be a prophet and a shepherd at the same time. Preaching and pastoral work, they point out, are so different that they may even counteract each other. This is accentuated by the trend toward specialization. In our large city churches, where a multiple staff is a necessity, one person may have primary responsibility for preaching; pastoral counseling and pastoral care are the responsibility of others who are not expected to do much, if any, preaching. It is further emphasized in the trend toward pastoral counseling specialists, men who are specially trained to do pastoral counseling and who may be serving on the staff of a church, or, on the other hand, as a chaplain in an institution, or in a counseling center, which may not be related to a church.

A certain amount of such specialization is inevitable in our urbanized culture. There are real values in specialized training. There are also some inherent dangers. If the pastor gives up his role as preacher, he loses one of his unique opportunities to serve. If the preacher assumes no responsibilities as pastor, he sacrifices insight into the needs of those to whom he preaches.

We grant that there are problems connected with maintaining both functions and recognize that there are some very real tensions between the two responsibilities, to the extent that they may even seem to be in conflict; yet, rightly conceived, we feel the two areas of responsibility strengthen and support each other. They each give to the other a uniqueness that is not found anywhere else. The relationship of preaching and pastoral work can perhaps best be seen in the experience and through the thoughts of some of those masters of another day and some of the authorities today who have given serious thought to the problem. We shall refer to some of them, dealing with them chronologically. This makes us aware that the problem really is not a new one at all.

Phillips Brooks is recognized as a great preacher, one of the greatest in fact. His Yale lectures on preaching, delivered in 1877, stand as a landmark in homiletic literature. In these lectures he was concentrating on preaching,

14

but he made frequent references to the work of the pastor. He said, "Every now and then somebody rises with a plea that is very familiar. . . . How much better it would be if only there could be a classification of ministers and duties. Let some ministers be wholly preachers, and some be wholly pastors." The problem is not new. He was talking even then about specialization.

He admitted the problem. He told the theological students they would find times when the two tasks would seem to be in "rivalry." He said there would be times when they would try to sit in the study and prepare a sermon but would be very conscious of the faces of the persons who needed their care. There would be other times when they would be among their people and feel guilty about the time they were not spending in the study. On such occasions, he said, they would wish they could be "either a preacher or a pastor, but not the two together."

But he continued and emphasized the fact that this is not a solution because "the two things are not two, but one. . . . The preacher needs to be pastor, that he may preach to real men. The pastor must be preacher, that he may keep the dignity of his work alive. . . . Be both; for you cannot really be one unless you also are the other."[1]

Just twenty years after Brooks gave his Yale lectures, John Watson (Ian Maclaren) appeared on the same platform. His theme is given in the title of his book *The Cure of Souls,* one of the first books to bear that title. This theme obviously places a great stress on the work of the pastor; in fact, it is one of the most eloquent statements on pastoral

---

[1]Brooks, *Lectures on Preaching* (New York: E. P. Dutton and Company, 1877), pp. 75-77.

work that had appeared until that time. Watson divided the work of the pastor, like that of the physician, into visitation and consultation. Much that he said anticipated later emphases in pastoral counseling and pastoral care.

He also spoke of preaching and reminded his hearers to remember "that the most critical and influential event in the religious week is the sermon." Like Brooks, he saw that the effectiveness with which he met people's needs in the pulpit depended to a large extent on how well he knew them as a pastor. Speaking of the preparation of the sermon he said, "Line by line the sermon has to be read over with the faces of his congregation before him, so that the minister may hear how it sounds in the living environment." Anything that was not relevant or that might hurt or harm must be deleted.

Furthermore, the minister must remember that the same people he sees during visitation and consultation are in the worshiping congregation.

Each man carries his own burden of unbelief, sorrow, temptation, care, into the House of God, and the preacher has to hearten all; . . . That minister who receives a body of people more or less cast down, and wearied in the great battle of the soul, and sends them forth full of good cheer and enthusiasm, has done his work and deserved well of his people. He has shown himself a true shepherd, and he has not done this service without knowing both the Will of God and the life of man, without draining a wide watershed of experience— from high hills where the soul has been alone with God, and from deep valleys where the soul has tasted the agonies of life—into the stream that shall be the motive power of many lives on the plains beneath.[2]

[2]Watson, *The Cure of Souls* (New York: Dodd, Mead & Company, 1896), pp. 3, 32, 5-6.

16

Charles Jefferson, pastor of the Broadway Tabernacle in New York, gave the George Shepard lectures at the Bangor Theological Seminary in 1904. He chose as his topic "The Minister as Prophet." He said:

The work of preaching is the most difficult of all the things which a minister is called to do. Indeed, it is the most difficult task to which any mortal can set himself. It is at once the most strenuous and the most exacting of all forms of labor. It requires a fuller combination of faculties and a finer balance of powers than are required in any other department of human effort.[3]

Eight years later he again gave the Shepard lectures at Bangor. This time he chose the theme "The Minister as Shepherd." In these lectures he said:

It is a work which requires extraordinary wisdom, unfailing patience, plodding fidelity, unfaltering boldness, a genius for hope, abiding faith, and boundless love, but there is none other that is more clearly the work that Christ just now wishes done, and upon the faithful performance of which the future of humanity more manifestly depends. The cities must be saved, and they are to be saved by shepherds.[4]

For Jefferson this was no contradiction. He firmly believed that a minister must be both prophet and shepherd and that the functions of each were, at the moment he was doing them, the most important thing he had to do. When Bishop Quayle wrote his book in 1910, he joined the two terms in the title and called it *The Pastor-Preacher*. He condemned as a "fallacy" the idea that a man cannot be both a preacher and a pastor. He said, "The axiom of a

---

[3]Jefferson, *The Minister as Prophet* (New York: Thomas Y. Crowell & Co., 1905), p. 6.

[4]Jefferson, *The Minister as Shepherd* (New York: Thomas Y. Crowell Company, 1912), pp. 94-95.

preacher's career should be, 'By the help of the great Pastor of the flock, I will be a pastor-preacher.' " His argument that it could be done was simply that *it had been done*. "Can a man do both pastoral and preaching work effectively? Certainly. And why speak so dogmatically on a disputed point? Because many ministers have done both." We would add that the men we have quoted bear out Quayle's argument. Brooks, Watson, and Jefferson were effective as preachers *and* as pastors. Quayle echoed the thought of Jefferson when he said, "Every faculty of soul, body, brain, spirit is brought into play when a preacher becomes a shepherd of souls."[5]

Harry Emerson Fosdick enjoyed the reputation in a later generation that Brooks enjoyed earlier, that of being the most widely followed preacher of his day. Fosdick, like Brooks, was also a great counselor. In the introduction to his book *On Being a Real Person,* a book which was written against a background of extensive counseling and with the problems of people such as those who had consulted him in mind, he said that when he began his counseling ministry, he announced "definite hours of conference when I would be available." He soon found himself overwhelmed, facing problems he didn't know existed and "fearing rightly that I might do more harm than good." Years later as he wrote this book he said, "As I look back on my ministry now, I wish that I could have extended my personal counseling farther, organized it better and handled it more competently. . . . Nothing in my ministry gives

---

[5]William A. Quayle, *The Pastor-Preacher* (Cincinnati: Jennings & Graham, 1910), pp. 22, 24, 27.

18

me more satisfaction now than the memory of some of the results."[6]

It was somewhat surprising in reading his autobiography, *The Living of These Days,* to discover that preaching also caused him some difficulty. Here he tells of his "struggle to discover how to preach," which went on "with no little perplexity." He tells that he used to envy some of his students who found preaching so instinctive and so natural. "Preaching for me," he said, "has never been easy, and at the start it was often exceedingly painful."

For him the solution was found when he saw the relationship between preaching and counseling. It was a gradual process, but when it became clear, the preaching became alive. He describes it in this way:

Little by little, however, the vision grew clearer. People come to church on Sunday with every kind of personal difficulty and problem flesh is heir to. A sermon was meant to meet such needs; it should be personal counseling on a group scale. If one had clairvoyance, one could know the sins and shames, the anxieties and doubts, the griefs and disillusionments, that filled the pews, and could by God's grace bring the saving truths of the gospel to bear on them as creatively as though he were speaking to a single person. That was the place to start—with the real problems of the people. That was a sermon's specialty, which made it a sermon, not an essay or a lecture. Every sermon should have for its main business the head-on constructive meeting of some problem which was puzzling minds, burdening consciences, distracting lives, and no sermon which so met a real human difficulty, with light to throw on it and help to win a victory over it, could possibly be futile.

---

[6]Fosdick, *On Being a Real Person* (New York: Harper & Brothers, Publishers, 1943), pp. vii-ix. Reprinted by permission of Harper & Row, Publishers.

For Fosdick such preaching included preaching for a decision—he expected results.

The preacher's business is not merely to discuss repentance but to persuade people to repent; not merely to debate the meaning and possibility of Christian faith, but to produce Christian faith in the lives of his listeners; not merely to talk about the available power of God to bring victory over trouble and temptation, but to send people out from their worship on Sunday with victory in their possession. A preacher's task is to create in his congregation the thing he is talking about.[7]

Turning from the men who have been known principally as preachers to those who have specialized in pastoral care, we find a similar emphasis. No one has made a greater contribution to the pastoral psychology movement than has Dr. Seward Hiltner. He sees the work of the minister not as different roles but as one role.

The pastor has several functions but one role. He carries out a variety of activities requiring several kinds of knowledge, but he works within one framework. His counseling and pastoral work, evangelism and missions, worship and preaching, religious and ethical education, administration and social action are not indications of fundamentally conflicting roles, but are inherent aspects of his performance of his role.[8]

In a book which he entitled *The Christian Shepherd* Dr. Hiltner says, "Shepherding, . . . does not describe the total function of the person we call a 'pastor.' He is also one who communicates the gospel and organizes the fellowship." In this book the minister's functions are divided into

---

[7]Fosdick, *The Living of These Days* (New York: Harper & Brothers, 1956), pp. 92, 84, 94, 99. Reprinted by permission of Harper & Row, Publishers.

[8]Hiltner, *Pastoral Counseling* (Nashville: Abingdon Press, 1949), pp. 169-170. Used by permission.

20

three categories— shepherding, communicating, organizing. "Each," Hiltner says, "under proper circumstances, becomes the principle concern."

He refers to the great commission of Jesus and its command to preach and to heal.

Both aspects of the commission are ways of presenting the gospel to the needs of men. They are not categorically different types of activity, nor do they have basically different aims. They are different ways of bringing what is absolutely needed to the hearts and minds of men, taking into account different situations, occasions, times, and needs. We should misunderstand the commission if we felt one aspect of it depends upon and is subsidiary to the other. Both preaching and healing are ways of linking the eternal gospel with specific need. Both are ways of performing the life-giving function. Neither, alone, is to be confused with the function itself.[9]

Wayne Oates in his book *The Christian Pastor* points out that there are some obvious differences in preaching and pastoral work, but he also stresses that there are some significant parallels. Whether one is thinking of his responsibility as a preacher or as a pastor, he must utilize the same laws of personality if he is to understand the people to whom he preaches or with whom he counsels. Both preaching and counseling depend upon a relationship, what Oates calls a "relationship of a trusted motive." Both depend on an understanding of feelings, and both require a growing understanding between pastor and people. Some problems obviously and of necessity can be dealt with only in the privacy and confidential relationship

---

[9]Hiltner, *The Christian Shepherd* (Nashville: Abingdon Press, 1959), pp. 19, 18. Used by permission.

of a one-to-one encounter. However, Oates points out, "the ministry of comfort and reassurance, instruction and interpretation, can often be done more powerfully through preaching than through individual counseling, because it is done in the presence of the larger community of worshipers."[10]

Howard Clinebell, in a recent book on *Mental Health Through Christian Community,* sees the sermon as one of the minister's "most valuable opportunities to enhance the mental and spiritual health of his people." The sermon provides a means whereby he can help "a number of individuals simultaneously." Thinking in terms of mental health, Clinebell sees the sermon as having "both preventive and therapeutic potentialities."

For relatively healthy persons it can stimulate personality growth and raise the general level of their creativity. It can release strength within those who are struggling with a personal crisis. It can support those whose personality foundations are weak, and motivate some who are burdened to seek professional help.

Clinebell sees the sermon as having many values.

Many people gain ego support by identifying with the preacher as he proclaims the great themes of wisdom and faith, courage and hope. . . . An effective sermon facilitates the renewal of trust by communicating the eternal verities of the faith within the supportive matrix of a religious community. . . . Person-centered preaching shares insights concerning common human problems and explores alternative ways of handling them.

---

[10]From *The Christian Pastor,* by Wayne Oates, p. 118. Copyright © 1951, 1964, W. L. Jenkins. The Westminster Press. Used by permission.

Clinebell says it is a common but erroneous assumption that there needs to be an "inevitable conflict between the pastoral and the prophetic, between counseling and preaching." He feels this results from a false dichotomy—"acceptance versus confrontation. Confronting a person with reality can be, in certain circumstances, the most accepting way of relating to him. This is equally true in preaching and in counseling."

Confrontation can be harmful, but when it consists of truth spoken in love, it can be creative. Being permissive and accepting does not mean a minister lacks convictions or does not stand for certain values. "A congregation which knows that their minister cares about them as persons will accept confrontation from him which they would automatically reject from another source."

Effective preaching, like effective counseling, depends upon "insight into life, nonjudgmentalism, warmth, and competence." It would be Clinebell's conviction that ministers "who take counseling seriously find that it deepens their preaching." Also, ministers who preach effectively will find it leads to counseling, for "a sermon can help an individual overcome his inner resistances to seeking help by strengthening his sense of need and by awakening hope that something can be done about his dilemma."[11]

We have quoted rather extensively from these men, for their thoughts and their experience bear a common testimony of the real possibilities that exist when one senses the inseparable relationship of the task of the preacher and the pastor. As Brooks said almost a century ago, "They are not two tasks but one."

---

[11]Clinebell, *Mental Health Through Christian Community* (Nashville: Abingdon Press, 1965), pp. 77-78, 83, 88, 85, 87. Used by permission.

Chapter 2

Preaching to Human Needs

One of the worst indictments that can be made against a sermon is that it wasn't relevant. No matter how well it has been prepared, no matter how scholarly its content, no matter how eloquently it was delivered, if it wasn't relevant, it had no value.

To state it more positively, all preaching worthy of the name must be relevant. This means it must be contemporary. It must draw on ancient truths, to be sure, but it must be addressed to people who are living now in a real world and must deal realistically with their personal and social needs.

All great preachers have been relevant to their day. They spoke to the needs, the concerns, and the problems of the people who listened. These people could relate the message to their world; they could apply it in their own lives. They saw its meaning for the day in which they lived. This was true of Amos as he spoke to the people of ancient Israel, of Peter on the Day of Pentecost, of Luther in Germany in the days of the Reformation, of Wesley as he addressed the miners at the mouth of the coal pits of England, of Whitfield as he spoke in log cabins in America. This was true of Robertson at Brighton, of

Baxter at Kidderminster, of Brooks in Boston, of Fosdick in New York. These men were relevant—they spoke to real needs.

Herbert H. Farmer tells how he checked himself when preparing a sermon so that this element would always be present. Speaking of a sermon, he said, "I have sometimes found it a help to write with a definite person in a definite situation before my mind's eye, putting to myself such questions as these, How would this sound to him? would he understand it? would it seem any other than an airy and irrelevant abstraction?"[1]

If a man is going to preach to personal needs, he has to know what the needs are. This means pastoral work. This means he must speak with understanding, the kind of understanding that comes only from involvement, from sharing the hopes and fears, the successes and failures, the sorrows and the aspirations of his people. One can get a list of human needs from a book. There are many such lists, and they are not without value. We are speaking of the kind of knowledge that comes only from experience. It comes not from reading about anxiety or fear but from patiently listening as someone pours out his anxieties, his doubts, his fears. It comes from sharing the life of those who are searching for meaning, hoping for some assurance of forgiveness, longing for faith.

This does not mean the preacher is excused from spending some time in the study or the library. On the contrary, it means he approaches such hours of study with a new earnestness and a deeper sense of need. Others, too, have grappled with human need. In autobiography and

---

[1]Farmer, *The Servant of the Word* (Philadelphia: Fortress Press, Preacher's Paperback Library, 1964), p. 81. Used by permission.

biography, psychology and sociology, literature and drama, we have the recorded wisdom of the race concerning human needs.

However, if a man merely reads books, he may become a scholar, but, if he separates himself from people, he will not become a preacher. Such a man is only a "book-preacher." His message may be good, it may be eloquent, but in the long run it will lack depth and reality. Merely to meet people face to face and to struggle with their problems is equally shortsighted. One may be aware of human needs by such a process, but he is dependent on his own wisdom for guidance and solutions. That is not enough. One who preaches to human needs must be a constant student of everything that increases his understanding of human behavior, and he must match his study with constant personal involvement.

If one is going to preach to human needs, he must saturate himself with the content of the Scriptures. Many people speak and write of human needs. Novelists describe them, psychologists analyze them, and sociologists categorize them. The preacher provides the spiritual solution as recorded in the Scriptures. This is his unique contribution.

Every need known to man is described in the Bible. Here is the record of the experience of a host of people described in stark realism. Here is the jealousy of Saul, the loyalty of Jonathan, the courage of Nathan, the despair of Jeremiah, the struggles of Paul—"I do not understand my own actions. For I do not do what I want, but I do the very thing I hate. . . . Wretched man that I am!" (Romans 7:15, 24).

26

Every emotion experienced by man is described in the Psalms. Here in the Scriptures are portrayed the results of such crippling emotions as guilt, doubt, futility, and fear, which warp and twist a life and disturb and destroy the soul. Here are also found the assurance of forgiveness, the belief in the value of each individual, the challenge to self-forgetful service, the message of the transforming power of love and of an unquestioning and unfaltering faith that make life strong and give it meaning.

If a man is going to preach to people's needs in general, he has to be willing to meet those people as individuals and to help them with their own unique and personal needs. It is unfair to raise a question of guilt in a sermon and then be unwilling to take the time to listen as a hearer comes to make a confession which was stimulated by that sermon. It is not right to urge men in public to have faith and then be unwilling to listen in private as someone pours out his own doubts and uncertainties. When preaching leads to such counseling, one function supplements the other, and the preacher-pastor is fulfilling his full responsibility and can be sure he is meeting real needs.

Dr. Herbert Farmer, quoted above, sees it as one task. "The act of preaching," he says, "is part of a larger system of personal relationships and cannot be rightly understood in separation from it. . . . In other words, preaching is essentially a pastoral activity. It is part of a pastoral relationship, one activity of a settled and continuous ministry."[2]

---

[2]*Ibid.*, p. 66.

Chapter 3

Preaching for Continued Growth

Dr. Gordon Allport wrote a book on the psychology of personality that has a title which is complete in one word —*Becoming.* This is a word that appears very frequently in the literature of both psychology and theology. Man, we are told, is in a constant state of becoming.

Seward Hiltner reminds us that "human growth does not follow a straight path. Put it on a graph and it would show up as an uneven line moving diagonally upward. The line would spurt up, flatten out, dip a little, then spurt upward again."[1] In all experience we make advances, hit plateaus, at times dip back a little, regroup our forces, and advance again. Of course, it is possible to go down instead of up. As Hiltner says, "The point at which we are on this line is not so important as whether the general direction is upward."[2]

All men need to be moving upward. All men need continued growth. Unless a man is making advances, he stagnates or slips back to a lower level. This growth may be very small, like the growth of a tree or even a flower. It

[1]Hiltner, *Self Understanding* (Nashville: Abingdon Press, 1951), p. 13. Used by permission.
[2]*Ibid.,* p. 18.

may be almost imperceptible, but it is nonetheless real. However, it does not just happen. This is where preaching is helpful.

Preaching can make a great contribution to meet this need to foster continued growth. Sometimes it does so by providing challenge, inspiration, and motivation. Without motivation there is no growth. Sometimes it accomplishes much by forcing a person to confront the evil in his life, to purge his soul of all that is unworthy and impedes his growth. Sometimes preaching fosters growth by providing information, knowledge, and understanding that enable someone to gain new insights and to see new meaning in life and the world.

This is not to deny the reality of sudden conversion or to discount dramatic, extensive advances. It is simply to recognize that a vast majority of people in the average Protestant congregation are going to advance gradually, little by little, one step at a time. Preaching can help them do so. This is what we call preaching for continued growth.

Such preaching is based on certain convictions. One has already been stated—growth is a basic human need. Another is that it is not only desirable but possible. The findings of educational psychology are very reassuring at this point. The old belief that learning was limited to the days of youth has been completely exploded. The learning curve may slow down a bit after the teen years, but it doesn't need to go down a very great extent. Again, the problem is one of motivation, and preaching is largely motivation. The Apostle Paul wrote late in his career, "Not that I have already obtained this or am already perfect; but I press on . . ." (Phil. 3:12). He was still growing.

If one is to preach for continued growth, he has to take into account people's present condition. The preacher has to begin where the people are if he is to lead them to higher levels. He also has to be conscious of, and to have faith in, what they can become. He has to be willing to help them *become*.

This is what Jesus did supremely. He saw people like Peter, James, and John, Mary Magdalene, Zacchaeus, and the woman by a well. He was well aware of their weaknesses and their sins—but he always saw them in terms of what they could be. "To all who received him, . . . he gave power to become . . ." (John 1:12).

The preacher must see this possibility for change—whether by sudden conversion or by gradual growth. Recognizing this possibility puts new purpose and meaning into many sermons. Dramatic change is wonderful when it is genuine and when it lasts; gradual growth is equally significant and miraculous. While we all take satisfaction in the sermon so dramatic and so powerful that it changes a life (although there were no doubt some forces at work prior to the sermon), we should never doubt or minimize the power of accumulated influence.

Is it the first or last blow which splits a rock? Both are necessary, in addition to many blows in between.

Faithful preaching based on human needs, an outgrowth of devoted study, and sincere prayer may provide an accumulated influence week in and week out, year in and year out, that results in much continued growth.

As we have said many times before, preaching and pastoral work cannot be separated. If we desire growth to take place in the lives of our people, it is not enough merely to preach about it. As pastors we also must be willing to work *with* the person who expresses a desire to grow.

This may well be a new emphasis in counseling. Thus far, counseling (pastoral and otherwise) has been concerned primarily with the disturbed, the maladjusted, the perplexed, the neurotic. This must be continued; such persons cannot be neglected. There is also the possibility that many people could be helped to live on a new level, to advance to a higher plateau of personal achievement, inner contentment, and greater usefulness if there were someone who was interested enough in their strivings to guide them, to make them aware of resources and possibilities, and to stand by them in the effort. This too is counseling. This too requires individual attention. This too must be based on individual needs, interests, and capacities.

Preaching and counseling supplement each other. They go hand in hand in challenging people and in guiding them in the process of continued growth.

Chapter 4

That They Might Become Saints

Carl R. Rogers, whose client-centered therapy has had such an extensive influence in counseling circles, recently published an article in which he discussed the kind of person he would expect to see as a result of a complete and successful therapeutic experience. He asks the question,

"If we were as successful as therapists as we could wish to be, what sort of persons would have developed in our therapy?"

Rogers believes such a person would "be open to his experience." He would be free from defensiveness. He would "live in an existential fashion. . . . Each moment would be new." Finally, "he would do what 'felt right' in this immediate moment and he would find this in general to be a competent and trustworthy guide to his behavior."[1]

If this is the person who would emerge if therapy were "maximally successful," an interesting question can be raised. What sort of person would emerge if preaching were maximally successful? What are the objectives and the goals of preaching?

The obvious goal of preaching is that people should become Christian or, in New Testament terms, that they might become saints. The word "saint" has been used in a different way throughout history. It has come to mean someone unique, someone who has been canonized and set apart, someone who is pictured in a stained-glass window. When the New Testament speaks of a saint, it is speaking of a very common person. The saints were the members of the Christian community. When Peter said he was going to visit the "saints" at Lydda, he was talking about very commonplace people (Acts 9:32). When Paul said, "Contribute to the needs of the saints," he wasn't talking about people who were in stained-glass windows, but people who were in need (Romans 12:13, 15:25). When he wrote, "All the saints greet you, especially those

[1] Carl R. Rogers, "The Concept of the Fully Functioning Person." *Psychotherapy: Theories, Research and Practice*, Vol. I, No. 1 (Aug., 1963). Used by permission of *Psychotherapy* and the author.

of Caesar's household" (Phil. 4:22), he was probably talking about slaves.

A saint, as we are using the term, is a person who has certain qualities of life and character. He is not a perfect person. He, too, knows the need for forgiveness. As one man said, "Even the saints had a past." Such a person may be famous like Augustine or Saint Francis, or he may be relatively unknown like the people at Lydda or Jerusalem.

What then are these qualities that make one a saint? William James in his classical book *The Varieties of Religious Experience* included a chapter with the simple title "Saintliness." When James was talking about saintliness, he was referring to certain qualities of character, qualities such as "charity, devotion, trust, patience and bravery," which he said were the result of religious ideals and religious experience. He quoted with approval Sainte-Beuve, who described a state of grace as "an inner state which before all things is one of love and humility, of infinite confidence in God, and of severity for one's self, accompanied with tenderness for others."[2]

This is a sentence which is so filled with meaning one will miss it unless he reads the sentence slowly and pauses to meditate and ponder it. Consider what it includes:

> —love
> —humility
> —confidence in God
> —discipline
> —tenderness for others

What more could one want for his people?

---

[2]James, *The Varieties of Religious Experience* (New York: Collier Books, 1961), pp. 211, 212.

If we prefer it in more modern psychological terms, we can find basically the same qualities in Abraham Maslow's description of self-actualizing persons. It is his contention that psychology until now has been very helpful in explaining sickness, neurosis, and weakness. Now we need to develop a psychology that explains health. The term he prefers for the healthy person is "self-actualizing." He says, "Self-actualizing people are altruistic, dedicated, self-transcending, social, etc. . . ."[3] These are basically the same traits of which William James spoke and which people in the New Testament experienced.

Maslow speaks much of "peak experiences." Peak experiences enable one to see clearly, to develop confidence, to live at one's best. Such experiences may not occur frequently, but when they do, they provide a sense of inner assurance, of freedom from doubt. They result in a creative, responsible, dedicated person.

Whether we prefer James' term "saintliness" or Maslow's "self-actualizing person," the goal is the same. Preaching should be so relevant to people's needs and of such sincerity and earnestness that it will enable people to have peak experiences. It should result in such experiences of insight, dedication, and genuine commitment that these "saintly" qualities will find expression in their lives.

---

[3]Maslow, *Toward a Psychology of Being* (Princeton, New Jersey: D. Van Nostrand Co., Inc., 1962), p. iii.

PART II

From Doubt to Faith

❧

From Guilt to Forgiveness

❧

From Hostility to Love

❧

From Restlessness to Peace

❧

From Pride to Humility

❧

From Childishness to Maturity

Through Discipline to Freedom

From Helped to Helper

From Doubt to Faith

❧ ❧ ❧

In almost any church on any Sunday, the preacher can be sure that various degrees of doubt and faith are present in the congregation. The people may all unite in singing "My Faith Looks Up to Thee," but this does not mean they all share a common faith. If the truth were known, a vast range of belief and disbelief would be present.

If any young people are in the congregation, the preacher can be almost sure that some of them are having problems with their religion. Adolescence is recognized as the traditional period of doubt. This is particularly true of those who are students in a college or university. Religious problems are accentuated on a college campus. The student must reconcile the religious faith of his childhood with all the findings of modern science, psychology, philosophy, and the other disciplines. This is not easy for anyone, and the student so often does not have adequate religious training to cope with these new issues. Of course, not all young people and students are troubled by doubt, but there are many who are.

The problem is by no means confined to students. Many older persons also have problems about doubt and faith. In every congregation there are people who ask questions about life's meaning or ask if it can have any meaning. There are some who have had experiences which have shaken their faith. As one person said, "I just don't know what to believe any more." There are some who feel their faith should mean more to them than it does. They say, "Others have found something here. Why can't I?" Some doubt is arrogant and cocky and hardly deserves consideration, but some doubt is wistful and searching. Many people come to church in the mood of the man in the Gospel of Mark who said, "I believe; help my unbelief!" (9:24).

Some of these persons find their way to the pastor's study. They seek him out for help. After all, the pastor is the one man in the community who is trained to deal with religious problems. In this area he should be a specialist. He is the one to whom other counselors should refer their clients and their patients when they express religious concerns. This means the pastor must know both counseling techniques and religious truth. Some religious problems are primarily emotional, some are theological. Some people need information, and others need to express their feelings of doubt and to share their problems with someone. They need to feel that someone understands. They do not need someone who will give them all the answers, but they do need someone who will stand by them in the search.

Much doubt comes to the pastor's attention in his regular round of pastoral responsibilities. As he ministers to people in time of sickness, trouble, and sorrow, he faces many problems of doubt and sees people grasping and struggling for faith, searching for something in which to believe.

It is out of such experiences that a pastor knows how real and all-consuming this problem can be. He knows that doubt can be very painful, that it is often accompanied by a sense of guilt. So many people have been taught that it is wrong to doubt that they compound the problem by adding guilt to the doubt. Some feel alienated or estranged from family and friends because they question some traditional beliefs. This often leaves them with a sense of loneliness, a feeling of being cut off from their past, of having lost something of value with nothing to take its place. It leaves them feeling insecure, with nothing in which to believe or trust.

The pastor also sees in his experiences the power of faith. He knows from his study of the Scriptures and from his experiences with people who have demonstrated the power of faith that it is a healing, sustaining, enriching power that results in courage, stability, and meaning. As one psychologist has said, a "basic trust" is the first requirement of a strong and healthy life.

To help people move from doubt to faith is the pastor-preacher's basic task. When a person comes with a problem of doubt, the pastor tries, of course, to help him. In the pulpit also he tries to help him and many like him, who may not have come for counsel but who have a similar problem.

Preaching offers the pastor-preacher a number of opportunities to be of real help.

(1) Through preaching he establishes his identity as a man of faith. Thus he becomes known both to the people and to other specialists who may refer people to him as one who has studied and understands the things of the spirit.

(2) Through preaching he makes a personal witness of his own commitment and his own convictions. It is precisely because he is a man of conviction, a man of faith, that people turn to him for help and advice.

(3) Through preaching he presents an image of one who would understand the doubter's problem, who would be appreciative of his concerns, who would be willing to help, and who in so doing would not be too judgmental, moralistic, or critical. (If he does appear judgmental, unsympathetic, and moralistic, he will probably be avoided and rightfully so.)

(4) Through preaching he can present a message of faith and can proclaim a gospel which is "good news," which does give courage and strength. Of all the many counselors, the pastoral counselor is the only one who appears before his people once a week with a message of faith.

(5) Through preaching he can supplement what he does in the interview. Some things can be accomplished better from the pulpit than in an interview. Since he does interpret faith from the pulpit, he is then free in the interview to listen and to let the parishioner vent his feelings and verbalize his concerns.

(6) Through preaching he can present the biblical teachings about the meaning of faith and the historic Christian doctrines that have been sources of strength for generations. Thus he can provide information which is so often sadly lacking in people's lives. It must be granted that a great deal of information cannot be included in a modern sermon of twenty to thirty minutes; yet it is surprising how much can be condensed into a sermon. Some people simply do not have the knowledge on which to base a faith—it is the preacher's task to provide such knowledge.

(7) Through preaching the pastor can provide the comforting assurance that all men of faith have had their struggles with doubts. There are few, if any, exceptions. The biblical characters all wrestled with the problem. The Book of Psalms is filled with references to a God who seemed "afar off" (Psalm 10:1), a God who seemed to hide his face (Psalm 13:1) from the people, as well as statements of confidence that the Lord was their shepherd. Luther was a man of faith, but he said, "Sometimes I believe, sometimes I doubt." So it was with Bushnell, Gladden, Fosdick, and all other men of faith. There is some reassurance in knowing that we are not the first ones to have faced the problem and that it is through facing such problems that a faith becomes one's own.

(8) Through preaching one can deal directly with some of the questions that are troubling men's minds. Dr. Fosdick did this repeatedly. If one will check through Fosdick's published sermons, he will find such titles as, "On Finding It Hard to Believe in God," "How Believe in a Good God

in a World Like This," "Religious Faith: Privilege or Problem," "When God Lets Us Down," "Having a Faith That Really Works," "The Importance of Doubting Our Doubts," "Christian Faith—Fantasy or Truth?"

(9) Through preaching the pastor can challenge people to make the venture of faith. In some areas of life, knowledge comes only through experience. Some things are not proved as much as they are experienced. Those who have made the "leap of faith" are those who have found they landed on solid ground. Those who have lived by faith are assured of faith.

In the two sermons that follow are illustrations of how two men have dealt with this issue. The first is a sermon from a generation or so ago. Bushnell himself went through an intense experience. He described it as a time of "agonies of mental darkness concerning God." Out of his own struggle he was able to help many others gain faith. The other sermon was preached to a contemporary audience in Old South Church in Boston, but it also was prepared to help people move from doubt to faith.

※

The Reason of Faith *

HORACE BUSHNELL

*"But I said unto you, That ye also have seen me,
and believe not."*—John 6:36

IT IS THE GRAND DISTINCTION of Christianity, that by which it is separated from all philosophies and schemes of mere ethics, that it makes its appeal to faith and upon

*From *Sermons for the New Life* by Horace Bushnell, copyright 1876, Charles Scribner's Sons.

that as a fundamental condition rests the promise of salvation. It is called the word of faith, the disciples are distinguished as believers, and Christ is published as the Saviour of them that believe.

But precisely this which is the boast of apostles is the scandal and offense of men. Were the word anything but a word of faith, a word of rhetoric or of reason or of absolute philosophy or of ethics or of grammar and lexicography, they could more easily accept it; but finding it instead a word of faith, they reject and scorn it. As if there were some merit or could be some dignity in faith! What is it but an arbitrary condition imposed to humble our self-respect or trample our proper intelligence? For what is there to value or praise, say they, in the mere belief of anything? If we hold any truth by our reason or by some act of perception or by the showing of sufficient evidence, what need of holding it by faith? If we undertake to hold it without such evidence, what is our belief in it but a surrender of our proper intelligence?

This kind of logic, so common as even to be the cant of our times, has all its plausibility in its own defect of insight, and nothing is wanting in any case to its complete refutation but simply a due understanding of what faith is, and what the office it fills. In this view I propose a discourse on the *reason of faith;* or to show *how it is that we, as intelligent beings, are called to believe; and how, as sinners, we can in the nature of things be saved only as we believe.*

I select the particular passage just cited for my text simply because it sets us at the point where seeing and believing are brought together; expecting to get some advantage, as regards the illustration of my subject, from the

42

mutual reference of one to the other as held in such prox-
imity. In this verse (the thirty-sixth) they are brought together as not being united, "ye have seen me and believe
not." Shortly after (in the fortieth verse) they are brought
together as being or to be united, "everyone that seeth the
Son and believeth on him."

Now the first thing we observe, for it stands on the face
of the language, is that faith is not sight, but something
different, so different that we may see and not believe. The
next thing is that sight does not, in the Scripture view, ex-
clude faith nor supersede the necessity of it, as the common
cavil supposes; for after sight faith is expected. And still
a third point is that sight is supposed even to furnish a
ground for faith, making it obligatory and, where it is not
yielded, increasing the guilt of the subject; which appears
both in the complaint of one verse and the requirement
of the other.

Thus much in regard to the particular case of the persons addressed, for they were such as had themselves seen
Christ, witnessed his miracles, heard his teachings and
watched the progress of his ministry. In that respect our
case is different. We get by historic evidences what they got
by their senses. The attestations we have are even more reliable evidences, I think, than those of sight; but they bring
us to exactly the same point: a settled impression of fact.
That such a being lived they saw with their eyes, and we
are satisfied that he lived by other evidences addressing our
judging faculty, as sight addressed theirs. We take their
case, accordingly, as the case proposed, and shape our
argument to it.

Suppose then that you had lived as a contemporary in
the days of Christ; that you had been privy to the dia-

logue between the angel and Mary, and also to all the intercourse of Mary and Elizabeth; that you had heard the song of the angels at the nativity, and seen their shining forms in the sky; that you were entirely familiar with the youth of Jesus, were present at his baptism, saw him begin his ministry, heard all his discourses, witnessed all his miracles, stood by his cross in the hour of his passion; that you saw him, heard him, ate with him, touched him after his resurrection and finally beheld his ascension from Olivet. You have had in other words a complete senseview of him from his first breath onward. What now does all this signify to you?

Possibly much, possibly nothing. If received without any kind of faith, absolutely nothing; if with two kinds of faith which are universally practised, it signifies the greatest fact of history; if with a third kind, equally rational and distinctively Christian, it signifies a new life in the soul and eternal salvation.

Let us, in the first place, look at these two kinds of faith which are universally practised; for if faith is, in the nature of things, absurd or unintelligent, we shall be as likely to discover the fact here as anywhere. And we may discover possibly that the very persons who discard faith as an offense to intelligence are not even able to do the commonest act of intelligence without it.

We begin then with the case of sight, or perception by sight. It has been, as some of you know, a great or even principal question with our philosophers for the last hundred years (and these are commonly the people most ready to complain of faith): How is it that we perceive objects? The question was raised by Berkeley's denial that we see them at all, which, though it convinced nobody,

44

objects through distances, and so have bridged the gulf between us and reality. Is then sight itself unintelligent because it includes an act of faith? Or if we believe in realities and have them by believing, would it be wiser and more rational to let alone realities, and live in figures and phantasms painted on the retina of our eyes?

But there is another kind of faith less subtle than this, which also is universally practised, and admitted universally to be intelligent. It is that kind of faith which, after sensation is passed or perception is completed, assigns truth to the things seen and takes them to be sound historic verities. Thus after Christ had been seen in all the facts of his life, it became a distinct question what to make of the facts; whether possibly there could have been some conspiracy in the miracles; some collusion or acting in the parts of Mary and her son; some self-imposition or hallucination that would account for his opinions of himself and the remarkable pretensions he put forth; whether possibly there was any mistake in the senses, or any sleight-of-hand by which they were imposed upon? Before, the difficulty was natural and related to the laws of sensation. Here it is moral, and respects the verity or integrity of the agents. For it is a remarkable fact that the mere seeing of any wonder never concludes the mind of the spectator. How many, for example, are testifying in our time that they have seen with their own eyes the most fantastic and extravagant wonders wrought by the modern necromacy; and yet they very commonly conclude by saying that they know not what to make of them; evidently doubting whether, after all, the sleight-of-hand tricks of jugglery, ventriloquism and magic, and the sometimes wondrous cunning of a lying character will not account for all they saw. These

46

doubts are not the ingenious doubts of philosophy, but the practical misgivings, questions and withholdings of good sense. And here again we perceive, as before, that the mere seeing of Christ concludes nothing in the spectator as regards his verity. He does not stand before the mind as a necessary truth of arithmetic or geometry; there the seeing ends debate, the mind is *ipso facto* concluded and there is no room for faith either to be given or withholden. As the philosopher doubted whether the objects seen had any real existence out of him, so the practical spectator doubts, after all Christ's wonders, whether everything was genuine, and the Christ who lived was just such a being as he seemed to be. Probably the evidence to one who saw was as perfect as it could be; but if we could imagine it to be increased in quantity and power a thousandfold, remaining the same in kind, the mere seeing would conclude nothing. All you could say in such a case would be that a given impression has been made, but that impression is practically naught, till an act of intellectual assent or credence is added on your part, which act of assent is also another kind of faith. If God were to burn himself into souls by lenses bigger than worlds, all you could say would be that so much impression is made, which impression is no historic verity to the mind till the mind assents, on its part, and concludes *itself* upon the impression. Then the impression becomes to it a real and historic fact, a sentence of credit passed.

We now come to the Christian or third kind of faith, with some advantages already gained. Indeed the argument against faith as an offense to reason, or as being insignificant where there is evidence, and absurd where there is not, is already quite ended. We discover in fact two degrees or kinds of faith going before and typifying and commending to our respect the higher faith that is to come after as a faith of salvation. We discover also that we cannot do even the commonest acts of intelligence without some kind of faith. First we complete an act of perception only by a kind of sense-faith, moving from ourselves and not from the objects perceived. Next we pass on the historic verity, the moral genuineness of what we see; and our act of credit so passed is also a kind of faith moving from us, and is something over and above all the impressions we have received. A third faith remains that is just as intelligent and in fact is only more intelligent than the others because it carries their results forward into the true uses.

This distinctively is the Scripture faith, the faith of salvation, the believing unto life eternal. It begins just where the other and last named faith ended. That decided the greatest fact of history: that Christ actually *was* according to all his demonstrations. It passed on the genuine truth of those demonstrations and set them as accredited to the account of history. Let everything stop at that point, and we only have a Christ, just as we have a Guatemozin or a Sardanapalus. The Christian facts are stored in history, and are scarcely more significant to us than if they were stored in the moon. What is wanted just here in the case of Christ, and what also is justified and even required by the facts of his life, is a faith that goes beyond the mere evidence of propositions or propositional verities about Christ—the faith of a *transaction;* and this faith is Christian faith. *It is the act of trust by which one being, a sinner, commits himself to another being, a Saviour.* It is not mind dealing with notions or notional truths. It is

48

what cannot be a proposition at all. But it is being trusting itself to being, and so becoming other and different by a relation wholly transactional.

If a man comes to a banker with a letter of credit from some other banker, that letter may be read and seen to be a real letter. The signature also may be approved, and the credit of the drawing party honored by the other as being wholly reliable. So far what is done is merely opinionative or notional, and there is no transactional faith. And yet there is a good preparation for this; just that is done which makes it intelligent. When the receiving party therefore accepts the letter and intrusts himself actually to the drawing party in so much money, there is the real act of faith, an act which answers to the operative or transactional faith of a disciple.

Another and perhaps better illustration may be taken from the patient or sick person as related to his physician. He sends for a physician just because he has been led to have a certain favorable opinion of his faithfulness and capacity. But the suffering him to feel his pulse, investigate his symptoms and make the diagnosis of his disease, imports nothing. It is only the committing of his being and life to this other being, consenting to receive and take his medicines, that imports a real faith, the faith of a transaction.

In the same manner Christian faith is the faith of a transaction. It is not the committing of one's thought in assent to any proposition, but the trusting of one's being to a being, there to be rested, kept, guided, molded, governed and possessed forever.

In this faith many things are presupposed, many included; and after it many will follow.

Everything is *presupposed* that makes the act intelligent and rational: that Christ actually lived and was what he declared himself to be; that he was no other than the incarnate Word of the Father; that he came into the world to recover and redeem it; that he is able to do it; able to forgive, regenerate, justify and set in eternal peace with God; and that all we see in his passion is a true revelation of God's feeling to the world.

There was also a certain antecedent improbability of any such holy visitation or regenerative grace, which has to be liquidated or cleared before the supposed faith can be transacted. We live in a state under sin where causes are running against us or running destructively in us. We have also a certain scientific respect to causes, and expect them to continue. But Christ comes into the world as one not under the scheme of causes. He declares that he is not of the world, but is from above. He undertakes to verify his claim by his miracles, and his miracles by his transcendent character. Assuming all the attributes of a power supernatural, he declares that he can take us out of nature and deliver us of the bad causes loosened by our sin. Now that he really is such a being, having such a power supernatural, able thus to save unto the uttermost, we are to have accredited, before we can trust ourselves to him.

But this will be less difficult because we are urged by such a sense of bondage under sin, and have such loads of conscious want, brokenness and helplessness upon us. Besides if we look again into our disorders, we find that they are themelves abnormal, disturbances only, by our sin, of the pure and orderly harmony of causes; so that Christ in restoring us does not break up, but only recomposes the true order of nature. Inasmuch therefore as our salvation

50

or deliverance from evil implies a restoration and not any breach of nature, the incredible thing appears to be already done by sin itself, and the credible, the restoration only, remains.

Having now all this previous matter cleared, we come to the transactional faith itself. We commit ourselves to the Lord Jesus by an act of total and eternal trust, which is our faith. The act is intelligent because it is intelligently prepared. It is not absurd, as being something more than evidence. It is not superseded by evidence. It is like the banker's acceptance and the patient's taking of medicine, a transactional faith that follows evidence.

The matters *included in* this act, for of these we will now speak, are the surrender of our mere self-care, the ceasing to live from our own point of separated will, a complete admission of the mind of Christ, a consenting practically to be modulated by his motives and aims, and to live, as it were, infolded in his spirit. It is committing one's character wholly to the living character of Jesus, so that every willing and working and sentiment shall be pliant to his superior mind and spirit; just as a man, trusting himself to some superior man in a total and complete confidence, allows that other to flow down upon him, assimilate him, and, as far as he may with a superiority so slight, conform him to the subject of his trust. Only there is in the faith of salvation a trusting in Christ vastly more interior and searching, a presence internal to parts internal, a complete bathing of the trusting soul in Christ's own love and beauty.

Those things which were just now named as presupposed matters are all opinionative and prior to this which is the real faith, and this faith must go beyond all mere historic credences of opinion; it must include the actual surrender of the man to the Saviour. It must even include the eternity or finality of that surrender, for if it is made only as an experiment, and the design is only to try what the Saviour will do, then it is experiment, not faith. Anything and everything which is necessary to make the soul a total, final deposit of trust in the Lord Jesus, must be included in the faith, else it is not faith, and cannot have the power of faith. It must be as if henceforth the subject saw his everything in Christ—his righteousness, his whole character, his life-work and death-struggle, and the hope of his eternity.

How great is the transaction! And *great results will follow,* such as these:

He will be as one possessed by Christ, created anew in Christ Jesus. There will be a Christ-power resting upon him and operative in him, an immediate knowledge of Christ as a being revealed in the consciousness. A Christly character will come over him and work itself into him. All his views of life will be changed. The old disturbance will be settled into loving order, and a conscious and sweet peace will flow down like a divine river through the soul, watering all its dryness. It will be in liberty, free to good, wanting only opportunities to do God's will. Fear will be cast out, confidence established, hope anchored, and all the great eternity to come taken possession of. Christ will constrain every motion in such a way that no constraint shall be felt, and the new man will be so exhilarated in obedience and raised so high in the sense of God upon him, that sacrifice itself will be joy, and the fires of martyrdom a chariot to the victor soul.

But the most remarkable, because to some the most unaccountable and extravagant result of faith, is the creation

52

of new evidence. The exercise of faith is itself a proving of the matter or the being trusted. It requires, in order to make it intelligent, some evidence going before; and then more evidence will follow of still another kind. As in trying a physician or trusting one's life to him, new evidence is obtained from the successful management of the disease, so the soul that trusts itself to Christ knows him with a new kind of knowledge that is more immediate and clear, knows him as a friend revealed within, knows him as the real power of God, even God in sacrifice. He that believeth hath the witness in himself: the proof of Jesus in him is made out and verified by trust. Everything in that text of Scripture that stumbles so many of our wise reasoners is verified to the letter: "Now faith is the substance of things hoped for, the evidence of things not seen." It is not said that faith goes before all evidence, but that, coming after some evidence, it discovers more and greater. It makes substance of what before stood in hope; it proves things unseen and knows them by the immediate evidence of their power in the soul. Hence it is that faith is described everywhere as a state so intensely luminous. Trust in God will even prove him to be, more inevitably and gloriously than all scientific arguments. The taking immortality by trust and acting one's mighty nature into it proves it, as it were, by the contact of it. The faith itself evidences the unseen life, when all previous evidences wore a questionable look. And so the whole Christian life becomes an element of light because the trust itself is an experience of Christ and of God.

And so truly intelligent is the process that it answers exactly, in a higher plane, to the process of perception itself already referred to. For when objects that cast their picture in the eye are accepted and trusted to as being more than pictures, as solid realities, then, by that faith is begun a kind of experiment. Taking now all these objects to be realities, we go into all the practical uses of life, handling them as realities. And so finding how they support all our uses and show themselves to be what we took them for, we say that we know them to be real, having found them by our trust. Exactly so it is, only in a much higher and nobler sense, that faith is the substance of things hoped for and the evidence of things not seen. Is there anything in this which scandalizes intelligence? I think not.

If now you have followed me in these illustrations, which I know are somewhat abstruse, you will not complain of their abstruseness, but will be glad by any means to escape from those difficulties which have been gathered round the subject of faith by the unilluminated and superficial speculations of our times. Handling the subject more superficially, I might have seemed to some to do more, but should in fact have done nothing. Let us gather up now, in closing, some of the lessons it yields.

1. The mistake is here corrected of those who are continually assuming that the gospel is a theorem, a something to be thought out, and now a new premise of fact communicated by God—by men to be received in all the threefold gradations of faith. To mill out a scheme of free will and responsibility, to settle metaphysically questions of ability and inability, to show the scheme of regeneration as related to a theory of sin and not to the conscious fact, may all be very ingenious and we may call it gospel; but it is scarcely more than a form of rationalism. Feeding on such notional and abstract wisdom, and not on Christ, the bread that came down from heaven, we grow at once

54

plainly there is no such thing as a raising of man without God; also that there is no God save as we find him by our trust, and have him revealed within by resting our eternity on him. And hence it is that all those Scripture forms of imputation spring up as a necessary language of faith under the gospel. We come in our trust unto God, and the moment we so embrace him by committing our total being and eternity to him, we find everything in us transformed. There is life in us from God; a kind of Christ-consciousness is opened in us, testifying with the apostle: "Christ liveth in me." We see therefore in him the store of all gifts and graces. Everything flows down upon us from him, and so we begin to speak of being washed, sanctified, justified in him. He is our peace, our light, our bread; the way, the truth, and the life. And in just the same manner he is our righteousness; for he is, so to speak, a soul of everlasting integrity for us, and when we come in to be with him, he becomes in us what he is to himself. We are new created and clothed in righteousness from his glorious investiture. The righteousness of God which is, by faith of Jesus Christ, unto all and upon all them that believe, is upon us, and the very instinct of our faith, looking unto God in this conscious translation of his nature to us, is to call him "The Lord our Righteousness, the justifier of him that believeth in Jesus."

Such now, my friends, is faith. It gives you God, fills you with God in immediate experimental knowledge, puts you in possession of all there is in him, and allows you to be invested with his character itself. Is such faith a burden, a hard and arbitrary requirement? Why, it is your only hope, your only possibility. Shall this most grand and blessed possibility be rejected? So far it has been, and you have even been able, it may be, in your lightness to invent ingenious reasons against any such plan of salvation. God forbid that you do not some time take the penalty of having to work out just that salvation without faith which you so blindly approve!

3. We perceive in our subject that mere impressions can never amount to faith. At this point the unbelievers and all such as are waiting to have convictions and spiritual impressions wrought in them that amount of faith, perfectly agree. The unbelievers and cavillers say that impressions, taken as evidences, are everything, and that over and above these faith is nonsense. You that are waiting to be in faith by merely having your convictions and feelings intensified, say the same thing, for you expect your impressions to coalesce in faith, and so to be faith. That, as we have seen already, is forever impossible. Faith is more than impression; it moves from you, it is the trusting of your being in a total, final act of commitment to the being of Christ, your Saviour. Impressions shot into you, even by thunder-bolts, would not be faith in you. "Ye also have seen me," says Jesus, "and believe not." No impression can be stronger and more positive than sight, and yet not even this was equivalent to faith. It was a good ground of faith, nothing more. Whatever drawings, then, impressions, convictions, evidences, God in his mercy may give you they will only ask your faith and wait for it. Will you, can you then, believe? On that question hangs everything decisive as regards your salvation. This crisis of faith—can you ever pass it, or will you always be waiting for a faith to begin in you which is not faith, and never can be? Let the faith be yours, as it must; your own coming to Christ, your own act of self-surrender, your coming over to him and eternal trust in him for peace, life, truth and bread;

knowing assuredly that he will be made unto you all these and more—wisdom, righteousness, sanctification and redemption.

Finally it is very plain that what is now most wanted in the Christian world is more faith. We too little respect faith, we dabble too much in reason; fabricating gospels where we ought to be receiving Christ; limiting all faith, if we chance to allow of faith, by the measures of previous evidence, and cutting the wings of faith when, laying hold of God and bathing in the secret mind of God, it conquers more and higher evidence. Here is the secret of our sects and schisms, that we are so much in the head; for when we should be one in faith, by receiving our one Lord, as soon as we go off into schemes and contrived summaries of notions reasoned into gospels, what can follow but that we have as many gospels as we have heads and theories? It never can be otherwise till we are united by faith. The word of reason is a word of interminable schism and subdivision, and the propagation of it, as in those animals that multiply by dividing their own bodies, will be a fissiparous process to the end of the world. O that the bleeding and lacerated body of Christ could once more be gathered unto the Head, and fastened there by a simple, vital trust! That his counsel and feeling and all his divine graces might flow down upon it, as a sacred healing and a vivifying impulse of love and sacrifice, and that so, fighting each other no more, we might all together fight the good fight of faith!

We shall never recover the true apostolic energy and be indued with power from on high, as the first disciples were—and this exactly is the prayer in which the holiest, most expectant and most longing souls on earth are waiting now before God—till we recover the lost faith. As regards a higher sanctification which is, I trust, the cherished hope of us all, nothing is plainer than the impossibility of it, except as we can yield to faith a higher honor and abide in it with a holier confidence. Every man is sanctified according to his faith, for it is by this trusting of himself to Christ that he becomes invested, exalted, irradiated, and finally glorified in Christ. *Be it unto you according to your faith* is the true principle, and by that the whole life-state of the church on earth always has been, always will be graduated. Increase our faith, then, Lord! Be this our prayer.

That prayer, I believe, is yet to be heard. After we have gone through all the rounds of science, speculation, dialectic cavil, and wise unbelief, we shall do what they did not even in the apostolic times, we shall begin to settle conceptions of faith that will allow us and all the ages to come to stand fast in it and do it honor. And then God will pour himself into the church again, I know not in what gifts. Faith will then be no horseman out upon the plain, but will have a citadel manned and defended, whence no power of man can ever dislodge it again. Faith will be as much stronger now than science, as it is higher and more diffusive. And now the reign of God is established. Christ is now the creed, and the whole church of God is in it, fulfilling the work of faith with power.

❊   ❊   ❊

The Impossibility of Unbelief*

FREDERICK M. MEEK

I

DURING RECENT YEARS the importance of Christian belief has been increasingly neglected, sometimes scorned, and frequently assailed as inconsequential or even harmful. The result is that our Protestant Churches in general have suffered immeasurable harm. The character of our people has been weakened. The spiritual life in our nation has been lowered. And because those abiding Christian beliefs about conduct and man and God, which are the root-soil of our democratic way of life at its best, have been missing from both our past deeds and our plans for tomorrow, we are a bewildered, perplexed people amid the competing philosophies and the many crises of our generation.

But men are so made that it is not possible to have the vacuum of unbelief at the center of any human life. Therefore in the lives of Christians and non-Christians the space once occupied by the great Christian beliefs could not for long remain empty. Inevitably other beliefs pushed their way through the doors of mind and heart and took up their residence at the center of our living.

In our self-sufficiency and in our preoccupation with developing material civilization, we said that Christian

*From *Monday to Friday Is Not Enough* by Frederick M. Meek, copyright 1951, Oxford University Press. Used by permission of the author.

belief in its demands and point of view was for a simpler day and that we did not believe. But we did! We simply had accepted other beliefs. And they directed our living. Unbelief is impossible! See what happened to us! See what came in to take the place once occupied by the great Christian beliefs!

We believed with naive abandon in the laws of the laboratory. It became Mt. Sinai; and some claimed to have heard a voice from amid the test tubes and the blinding lights saying, "Thou shalt have no other God before me." And there were times when the multitudes bowed down and said: "Thou art my rock and my salvation!" We still believed. We had simply exchanged our goods—a greater God for a lesser idol—a loving, powerful, wise, redeeming God for secondhand impersonal forces, which we had learned partially to handle.

We believed without question in the unseen powers of electricity and atomic fission, but not in the unseen, equally observable powers of prayer (men talking to God and God talking to men) working in human life.

We believed completely in ourselves and in what we could do. It was our substitute for the infinite love and understanding of the Father of our Lord Jesus Christ, which we had relegated to the historical archives. ("See the curious things which men once possessed and used!")

We believed the extravagant claims of the multicolored advertisements and took them as our guide for living, putting their will-o'-the-wisp direction in the place of the Christian faith and experience which says: "A man's life consisteth not in the abundance of the things which he possesseth."

We believed in the powers of evil (and we ought to

61

know, because no generation has seen more sheer human horror and evil than ours has since 1914). And we still plan life on the basis of a belief that the powers of evil are stronger than the powers of God's great good. (Listen to any session of the American Congress or the United Nations.) We believe in the usefulness of expediency and in the importance of temporary desire, but we do not believe in the eternal abiding standards of Christian conduct.

We still believe in Jesus (somehow we cannot escape Him). But we believe on our own terms in a wise and kindly figure, flatteringly like ouselves in our better and more amiable moments. But we do not believe in a Christ who was unique—The Son of God among the sons of God—in whom God showed Himself and His salvation most clearly to us and all men.

II

Thus the recent story of the religious life of us Americans and of millions of people in our Protestant churches is the record of the gradual denaturing of Christian belief, of eliminating everything that did not fit the pattern of our immediate secular experience, of omitting everything that would make the word about God God-like instead of man-like. We wanted the story of the New Testament to fit the dimensions of any average human biography or story which a good writer would set down, hoping that the critics would find the story interesting and believable.

The thought that there was anything about Almighty God, the Creator of the complexities of existence in time and eternity, that might cause us to wonder, or that might not be understood completely by our little minds, was regarded as superstitious and questionable. And sometimes we called our attitude "open-minded liberalism." Sometimes the minds were open at both ends and they held nothing!

In religious education we emphasized methods and techniques of teaching, and we were poverty-stricken in the content of the Christian Gospel which we imparted to our children and young people.

Mildred McAfee Horton said, several years ago, that about 98.8 per cent of her students entered Wellesley College with some church affiliation, and that approximately the same proportion were essentially ignorant of the religious tradition to which they claimed allegiance.

We had a self-conscious timidity about expressing any specifically Christian Protestant point of view. In interfaith gatherings, it was perfectly in order for a Jew or a Catholic to state frankly and unashamedly what he believed; but it was considered bad taste and intolerant for a Protestant to admit in public that he really believed anything that differentiated him and his history from these two traditions. And so amiable goodwill, without the sinew of belief, gave no offense as it discarded the distinctive features of Protestantism.

We wanted nothing at the center of our living that could not be handled with the ease and certainty of a problem in elementary arithmetic; we wanted nothing that could not be understood by our own unaided senses and limited minds; we wanted nothing that was not "natural," i.e. man-limited and man-contained; we wanted nothing to do with the "supernatural," i.e. with the greatness and the mystery of God; we wanted nothing that did not center in the here and the now (except occasionally when death came to some loved one, and of ourselves we had neither

63

understanding nor strength nor consolation). Accordingly the Gospel was interpreted in terms of the man-centered man-manipulated sciences, psychology and sociology. And we brushed aside the science of theology: that logical sustained thought about the great mystery and problems of living in the light of God and His existence, and what He does and purposes.

The result was a meager poverty of Christian experience and faith without power and without salvation, an experience confined to the little that man can do for himself in his awful predicament.

III

How different is such inadequacy from the experience of power shared in by Christians in generations marked by positive belief. Their deepest satisfaction was found in being able to say as Christian people: "I believe." They rejoiced in their affirmations. And as these affirmations worked their power in and through them, they brought strength and wisdom sufficient to do those Christian deeds of individual heroism and world significance which still glow on the dull printed page. They knew at first hand the experience of the words of our text. They knew "the greatness of His power to us who believe."

But our condition of unbelief—lack of Christian belief—has had far-reaching consequences. We have been brought collectively to the edge of the pit, and individually into the quicksands of confusion. We Western peoples, unguided by great beliefs about man and God and life, are the key figures in the disastrous human defeat of the events and wars of the last thirty years, followed now by a future prospect which, if limited to our wisdom, is of unrelieved gloom and inevitable catastrophe.

This defeat, both in its individual and collective aspects, is directly traceable to the Christian failures of us Western people, to whom the Christian Gospel first came from the apostles and the early followers. In later days we perverted the Gospel, as, for example, did the peoples of pre-revolutionary Russia in their corrupt Church, as did the peoples of Italy and Spain when the Church became a parasite, battening upon the people. Or we discarded the Gospel for some primitive faith of blood and soil and nationalism as did the people of Germany, or for a completely secular life as did the people of France. Or we kept the Christian forms and said the words and denied the spirit, as did the English-speaking world of the United States and Great Britain, both of whom are now faced by the rise of a powerful, spiritually illiterate generation, whose way of life cuts the very roots from our democratic institutions. The greatest source of weakness in the English-speaking world is our spiritual illiteracy.

The circumstances which we face are pointed up by an experience related by a well-known literary figure. He wrote: "We invited many of our misfortunes when we threw overboard much of the cargo (of codes and standards) of behaviour we had accumulated on the long voyage from barbarism. We lightened the ship, but ships and hearts may become too light for safety. The riskiest and most uncomfortable journey I ever made was across the mid-winter Atlantic in a freighter loaded with cork. That boat sped almost as fast as the wind behind her, and danced like a debutante but everything aboard her was smashed, and she narrowly escaped foundering. We have gone lightly and swiftly through recent years, but we, too, have narrowly escaped foundering. There is a good deal of ballast it is better to carry for comfort and caution."[1]

The seas ahead are rougher and more tempestuous than anything through which we have yet come. At present we are at anchorage before the next stage of our voyage in time and eternity. The ship itself is seaworthy, but it needs the ballast of the great beliefs of our Christian faith. Not until those beliefs are part of our cargo can we face the prospect of the future journey with any degree of equanimity and surety.

IV

Our great difficulty arises from the inadequacy and half-heartedness of our belief about God, the sustaining creating Architect of our world, and the Father of you and me and of the multicolored diverse humanity. If we Christian people gave the same kind of persistent and at times intelligent effort to understanding what He purposes about life and its destiny that we do to understanding the problems of our individual business, of our household management, or of our children's education, the resulting convictions and beliefs and deeds would be strong enough to create new people and a new world.

But, curiously enough, a strange human inertia stands in the way. There is an unwillingness to take the time or make the effort to become familiar with the facts and experiences of the Christian Gospel as the Christian Gospel, and not as the secular denatured substitute which so many of us have adopted and named falsely "Christianity."

---

[1] Channing Pollock, *Guide-Posts in Chaos* (New York: Thomas Y. Crowell Company, Publishers, copyright 1942 by Channing Pollock), p. xv.

I would that it were within my power to have this letter, written by Miss Dorothy Sayers of mystery-story fame, read in every church and public assembly in America. Here it is as she wrote it to be read to the people of the City Temple in London. She writes:

The only letter I ever want to address to "average people" is one that says,—

Why don't you take the trouble to find out what is Christianity and what isn't? Why, when you can bestir yourselves to mug up technical terms about electricity, won't you do as much for theology before you begin to argue about it? Why do you never read either the ancient or modern authorities in the subject, but take your information for the most part from biologists and physicists, who have picked it up as inaccurately as yourselves? Why do you accept mildewed old heresies as bold and constructive contributions to modern Christian thought, when any handbook on Church history would tell you where they come from? Why do you complain that the proposition "God is Three-in-One" is obscure and mystical, and yet acquiesce meekly in the physicist's "fundamental formula," "$qp - pq = ih/2\pi$, where $i = \sqrt{-1}$," when you know quite well that $\sqrt{-1}$ is paradoxical and π incalculable? What makes you suppose that the expression "God ordains" is narrow and bigoted anthropomorphism, whereas the expressions "Nature provides" or "science demands" are objective statements of fact? Why, when you insist on the importance of being modern and progressive, do you never read any textual criticism of the Bible that is not fifty years out of date; and why, on the other hand, when you insist on going back to the "pre-Pauline simplicity of the Gospels," does it never occur to you to verify your dates and discover which came first, the Gospels or St. Paul? Why don't you do a hand's turn for yourselves, confound you? You would be ashamed to know as little about internal combustion as you do about the Nicene Creed. I admit that you can practise Christianity without knowing much about theology, just as you can drive a car without understanding internal combustion—but if something breaks down in the car, you go humbly to the man who understands the work, whereas if something goes wrong with your religion you merely throw the creed away and tell the theologian he's a liar. Why do you want a letter from me telling you about God? You will never bother to check up on it and find out whether I am giving you a personal opinion or the Church's doctrine, and your minds are so confused that you would rather hear the former than the latter. Go away and do some work, and let me get on with mine.

Yours very sincerely,
Dorothy L. Sayers[2]

People in Protestant churches all over America will find their attitudes aptly described by Miss Sayers' communication.

V

What then are the beliefs to which the Christian Gospel asks our assent and in the light of which we must live? Obviously in the latter part of a sermon addressed to Christian people on the necessity of Christian belief, there is only the opportunity (which is an obligation) to point to the horizons to which we must go.

To say, and actually to put it at the heart of our living, "I believe in God, the Father Almighty" is the greatest of all the experiences that can come to you and me. It is to know that He is the source from which our living comes and in which our strength and wisdom are found. It is to say that here is the standard by which the right and the wrong of our living are to be judged. It is to gather up

---

[2]Dorothy Sayers, "Letter to the Average People," *The City Temple Tidings.*

everything: our loves, our homes, our leisure hours, our business and our accounts, and to say to Him who had a thought for you and me in the eternal counsels of His will: "How am I doing? Is this the way that You want it done?" See what this could do to bring order into life. Imagine a nation of people living in this way! Therein is the answer which mankind is seeking.

If we have such a belief in God the Father Almighty, then the evil of life and not the good is the problem. The evil of life is the fact with which every religion and philosophy of life has struggled, but the Christian Gospel says that in the Cross-experience of Jesus the Christian answer comes with dramatic force. Its word is that God knows, that God is with us even in the depths of the evil and sorrow, and that out of His companionship men can endure and eventually can go on to a new and more adequate life. Here Christianity offers an explanation in part, but beyond that it offers the possibility of something better than an explanation, a strategy of living in the midst of the worst.

If we balk at affirming "I believe in God the Father Almighty," then the good, the best, our loves and hopes and fine deeds, become the inexplicable problem; we assume a world in which evil and suffering and sin are finally all-powerful, and the good is only accidental; a world without final hope or ultimate reason, in which the deeds of opportunism of a Hitler or a Goering, of a Bilbo or a Frank Hague, or a Kelly-Nash machine in Chicago (to come no nearer home) are justified, because there is no final and ultimate justice or moral order to oppose their cruelty and expediency.

This Christian affirmation, "I believe in God the Father

69

Almighty" is the most reasonable of all beliefs; and for many of us it rests on the second great Christian belief.

VI

The second great belief is this: "I believe in Jesus Christ." This is New Testament Christianity. In Jesus there is something unique. In Him, once and for all, we have been shown what God Almighty can do within the pattern of our human life when given a chance. Jesus is the first of the new race of men. It is only right that time should be divided by his existence into "before" and "after," into B.C. and A.D., for here God acted decisively and dramatically to give His most understandable clues to Himself and to His purpose. And most important He showed more than reason and justice; He showed that He is loving and affectionate and forgiving toward us. If there be no understanding and no forgiveness, then we in our failures are lost, and we had better quit this business of existence now; for see what havoc we make of our world and of ourselves. But God still stands beside, ready to forgive and to aid the sincerely penitent seeker, even as does the best parent whom we know. Do we really believe that? If we do, then we are not without hope. And when we say we believe in Jesus Christ, we are turning our faces in the direction in which time itself is going; for eventually there will be that new race of men of which He was the first.

VII

From these two great affirmations stem the whole Christian Gospel and its life-embracing experiences: Christmas, Holy Week, Good Friday, Easter Sunday, the Sermon on the Mount, the New Testament writings, the growing body of Christian experience of the past two thousand years, all making an inseparable, integral whole.

When these beliefs are put into the language of our time, and their connection made plain with the circumstances which we and our generation confront, then the Christian Gospel becomes the guiding saving force for us and our bewildered frightened age.

It is impossible to exaggerate the hazards which have to be faced by each of us. If we face them with the direction of the prevailing secular and ofttimes pagan philosophy which guides so many people, our beliefs about life and man and our world and God will shrink until they are small enough to fit the bleak prospect of an ultimate defeat. But if we and our time are in touch with the faith and courage, the wisdom and power of this Christian Gospel, with its word from and about God, then in place of the average man's secular despair there will come alive those Christian hopes and strategies which will be for the saving of man and of nations.

In J. B. Priestley's novel, *Daylight on Saturday,* Sammy (a workman) is despairing because ". . . people 'aven't much to get 'old of. They feel a bit empty inside. They don't know 'where they're goin' or what it's all about. An' nobody an' nothin' tells 'em." The superintendent says, "Surely there are plenty of chaps ready to tell them where they're going or what it's all about—parsons, professors, writers, and so on." Sammy answers, "But I fancy most o' them don't know neither. If they did an' were certain, they'd come runnin' wi' the good news. An' people'll listen all right if a proper message comes through."[3]

---

[3] J. B. Priestley, *Daylight on Saturday* (New York: Harper and Brothers, 1943), p. 208. Used by permission of the author.

If you and I have at the heart of our living those Christian beliefs which are the valid good news for our time, we will come running to tell other people. And other people will listen, for they really want to hear. If Christian people have such convictions, then once more we will become a witnessing people, moving men and events Godward. In the end it becomes the most personal matter in the world. Behind our work, our hours of recreation, our friendships and our loves, behind casual conversations and political judgments, lie the beliefs upon which we are betting our lives and the existence of our generation. Are they Christian? Behind our tear-dimmed eyes in an hour of grief, behind the fear of failure and the numbing experience of defeat, lies the power of the beliefs which are at the core of our living. Are they Christian? Behind our hopes for ourselves and our children and our nation lie our beliefs about life and its destiny. Are they Christian? The character of tomorrow's events, and of tomorrow's you and me, depends upon what we believe about God and His purpose. Is it Christian? If our beliefs are rooted in the Christian Gospel, then we too will know "the greatness of His power to us who believe."

From Guilt to Forgiveness

❧ ❧ ❧

Dr. Paul Tournier, noted Swiss physician and lay theologian, wrote, "There is no worse suffering than a guilty conscience, and certainly none more harmful."[1] He cites numerous cases from his medical practice of people who had no discernible medical problems, but who developed all kinds of physical symptoms. Their lives had become almost intolerable because of a sense of guilt.

A sense of guilt can literally wreak havoc in a man's soul. Nothing is right if a man feels guilty inside. Playwrights and novelists have always known this. Shakespeare described it in *Macbeth,* as Hawthorne did in *The Scarlet Letter.* There are many examples of it in the Bible. More recently, psychiatrists have been making us acutely aware of the destructive power of guilt.

Just as the pastor may be sure that in every congregation there are some people troubled by doubt, he can be equally sure that there are some people experiencing guilt. This is probably good to a certain extent. All men should be conscious of their need for forgiveness. "All have sinned and fall short of the glory of God," the New Testament tells us (Romans 3:23). That is an all-inclusive statement. It includes the entire congregation. The Bible also says, "If we say we have no sin, we deceive ourselves, and the truth is not in us" (1 John 1:8). All men need forgiveness. Some who come to

[1]Tournier, *A Doctor's Casebook in the Light of the Bible,* trans. Edwin Hudson (American ed.; New York: Harper & Brothers, 1960), p. 210.

church are aware of it. They are haunted by a sense of guilt and unworthiness; their very presence may be due to their seeking some solution, some relief. On the other hand, some people may be quite unaware that they, too, need repentance and forgiveness.

Those who are troubled and disturbed by their guilt come with very responsive minds. They need some solution. They have probably already tried many things. Some have tried to suppress their guilt, or, worse, to repress it, to bury it, to deny it exists, only to discover they can't get rid of it this way. It reappears as insomnia, anxiety, disease.

Some try to rationalize it away and say, "I can't be so bad because there are others who are worse." Some try to shift the blame, to project it on others. "It really wasn't my fault," they say. Some become overly critical of others. If they can find flaws in others, their own wrong doesn't seem quite so bad.

Some try to forget their guilt in an endless round of activity. It may be in a mad search for pleasure or in excessive work. Some try a self-imposed penance. They may punish themselves in some way; they may give to worthy causes; they may do many good deeds—but in the long run none of these is effective. Pleasure, activity, and good works do not provide forgiveness.

Many of these people come to the pastor's study when the burden has become unbearable. They have to find some solution. The Protestant pastor has no confessional where he hears confessions and pronounces absolution, but he, nevertheless, hears many confessions. Sometimes such confessions come in the midst of pastoral responsibilities. A pastor may be making a call in the hospital when a patient may confess some wrong committed twenty years ago. He never would have come to the pastor's study. He had managed to suppress the feeling, to endure it through the years, but now as he has time to ponder many things, he can endure it no longer.

The pastor faces no more delicate or sacred responsibility

than when he hears a confession and attempts to help a person move from guilt to forgiveness. For some people the confession may be enough, but for others it may need to be followed by extensive counseling, even referral to another source of help. The pastor knows when he preaches on guilt and forgiveness that there are some people in the congregation for whom this is the central issue in their lives. It is keeping them awake at night. It endangers their health and destroys their happiness; their future and their ultimate salvation depend on finding a solution.

For this reason all such preaching must be done with the greatest of care. Words like "sin," "guilt," "remorse," "shame," "repentance," "unworthiness," and "forgiveness" are emotional, highly charged words. The pastor ought not to preach on such subjects unless he makes his preparation with great care. He has no right to speak about repentance unless he is willing to give the time to an individual who may desperately need to repent, who is willing to make a confession, and who hopes for a chance to make restitution. Some cases can be handled only in the privacy of the counseling interview.

Much can be done through preaching.

(1) Through preaching the pastor can present the biblical teachings on sin, repentance, guilt, forgiveness, and redemption. An expression of confession is found, for example, in Psalm 51. The first chapter of 1 John and the teachings of Jesus are also filled with the message of guilt and forgiveness.

(2) Through preaching the pastor can teach the doctrine of forgiveness. Although guilt has many psychological ramifications, basically it is a religious problem. This is the heart of the gospel message. Man has sinned, but God reconciles, forgives, pardons.

(3) Through preaching the pastor can assure people of the possibility of gaining forgiveness. This is the great good news which applies to all members of the congregation. They need not continue to be burdened by guilt.

(4) Through preaching the pastor can make clear the steps in attaining forgiveness, not in some over-simplified manner, but by interpreting the need for, and the meaning of, repentance and confession.

(5) Through preaching he can point out the need to develop a forgiving spirit and to make restitution when possible. The Sermon on the Mount reads, "If you do not forgive men their trespasses, neither will your Father forgive your trespasses" (Matthew 6:15). It is a spiritual law of life that we cannot receive what we refuse to give. Those who love receive love; the merciful obtain mercy. Even God cannot enter a life that harbors a bitter and unforgiving spirit.

(6) Through preaching the pastor can distinguish between real guilt and neurotic guilt, between deserved guilt and undeserved guilt. Some people feel guilty for events over which they had no control or for actions which were not really wrong. They probably need counseling more than preaching, but preaching can help.

(7) Through preaching the pastor can make people aware of their need of forgiveness. This must be done with great care. Psychiatrists are rightly critical of the church for arousing unnecessary, undeserved feelings of guilt. The fact remains, as the Scriptures say, that all men need forgiveness. "If we say we have no sin, we deceive ourselves, . . ." (1 John 1:8). Not all are guilty of the sins of the flesh, but many in the congregation are guilty of the sins of the spirit, such as attitudes of intolerance, prejudice, and bitterness. There exist the great ills of society for which we all bear a responsibility. There are the sins of neglect. It isn't always the things we have done that are wrong—but the things we failed to do, the burden we neglected to share, the service we did not render. Guilt can be wholesome—it can lead to growth.

(8) Through preaching a man presents an image of himself. As we said in the section on doubt and faith, if the preacher presents himself as one who would be judgmental, censorious,

and moralistic, he presents himself as one who would not understand, and the person in the pew will say to himself either consciously or unconsciously, "This is a man I want to avoid." On the other hand, if the preacher presents the image of one who does understand, who himself shares the frailties of life, and if he identifies himself with his people, but always with a faith in One who forgives and redeems, then people will say, "This is one who could help me."

(9) Through preaching the pastor helps people gain faith in a God who forgives and, more important, who is willing to forgive them, so that they can make confession and accept forgiveness, secure in the trust that

> . . . as far as the east is from the west,
>   so far does he remove our transgressions from us.
>
> —Psalm 103: 12

> For thou, O Lord, art good and forgiving,
>   abounding in steadfast love to all who call on thee.
>
> —Psalm 86:5

❧

The Forgiveness of Sins *

GEORGE ADAM SMITH

*The forgiveness of our sins according
to the riches of His grace*—Ephesians 1:7

I WISH TO SEEK with you some of the answers, to be found in the Scriptures and our own experience, to the question: In what does the forgiveness of sins consist? There is another question inseparable from this, and of

---

*From *The Forgiveness of Sins* by George Adam Smith, copyright 1904, A. C. Armstrong & Son.

77

equal importance with it: How is the forgiveness of sins assured to us? To which the answer is: Through the perfect sacrifice offered once for all in the life and death of Jesus Christ, the Son of God. We shall carry this answer with us, and before we are done we shall consider what it does to enhance the meaning and obligations of forgiveness. But our main purpose is to ask what that meaning is. We do not aim at a historical survey or systematic statement of Bible doctrine on the subject. It is only some practical answers we seek—I do not pretend they are exhaustive—from the Bible as well as from our own experience to one of the most urgent questions which that experience presses upon us: In what does the forgiveness of sins consist?

I

The strongest proofs of the need of forgiveness, or, in other words, of the reality of the sense of sin, have been found by some observers in the universality of that sense, or at least in the fact, which the dramatists of all ages have treated as the most certain and tragic element in human experience—the persistence and ineradicableness of a sense of guilt: the hopelessness of outrunning conscience, however successfully some versatile men may have appeared to do so, upon their passions, or upon a strong ambition, or upon the cleaner carriage of an intellectual pursuit, or a busy service of their fellows. Neither the most powerful nor the most pure absorptions, of which the heart is capable, are of themselves sufficient to redeem a man from the conscience of a selfish, a cruel, or a cowardly deed. I need not linger to remind you of how fully the Bible illustrates and enforces these conclusions of our experience.

78

But more convincing that this inevitableness of conscience by all men, however hardy and reckless, is the fact that the sense of sin appears most keen and painful in the purest and the truest hearts: that it is the most holy of our race, who have most acutely felt their guilt and need of forgiveness. Which of us can remain unashamed in presence of the shame of the Saints? With that shame also the Bible is red. The verses which burn with it, the Psalms, which are blotted with its tears or broken by its sobs, are today and for ever will be, the confessional of humanity. Do not think that it is where the criminal or the murderer breaks down in confession that we will *most* keenly find our conscience. It is the saints upon their knees who draw us beside them; where Isaiah feels his lips unclean before the Throne; where Peter falls at the feet of Christ; where Paul cries crushed and broken from the captivity that is upon him; where John looks us in the face and says: *If any man say that he has no sin he deceiveth himself and the truth is not in him.*

But indeed we do not require to go beyond our own experience. Abstract and pale are the evidences of sin in other men besides those with which each of us can furnish himself. If you and I are awake to-day and if we are dealing honestly with ourselves there is not one of us who cannot find in his own memory and by his own conscience infinitely more painful proofs of the need of forgiveness than the most reckless or the most holy lives of others can possibly present to him. *If any man say that he have no sin he deceiveth himself and the truth is not in him.*

I know that I am speaking to many who are at a stage of life when all this can hardly have the same force as it will when you are older. In our youth religion attracts us more by the ideals and aspirations with which she inspires our strength, than by the remedies and reliefs which she offers to our weakness. But as the years go on it is the sense of the need of forgiveness of which we become most aware. It is an older man who says: *Remember not the sins of my youth, O Lord, nor my transgressions: but according to thy loving kindness remember thou me.* We have missed opportunities, we have neglected duties. Whatever good use we have made of some of the relations of life, there are others which we have wasted, or to which through selfishness we have been utterly blind. We have not been fully loyal to the hearts that loved and trusted us. We have gone astray in face of manifest warnings from on high. We have sinned against the light and love of God our Father. The years do not lessen nor wear thin this sense of guilt. Rather they bring out all the colour that is in it: red and awful to our eyes. Every additional one teaches us that it is the most inseparable element of human experience, perhaps to be thrown off by nimble youth, but certain to make up on later years. Guilt, a bad conscience, remorse— it is not our theologians but our poets and depictors of human life who have vied with each other in showing how these stick to a man, and how though he carry nothing else out of life with him he carries this. *The sting of death is sin.* "It is like a piece of bad workmanship," one of our greater English novelists makes one of her characters, a carpenter, say: "It's like a piece of bad workmanship, you never, never see the end of it."

Yet the Prophets made it one of their principal proclamations that God forgave the sins and removed the guilt of the penitent; and Christ went further and announced that the removal of the guilt of men was His work and the

ment in its most material form whether here or hereafter; and by such natures forgiveness will therefore be
sought and expected as the remission of the material consequences of a man's misdeeds. But penitence of this kind
is surely little more than the sorrow of the world which
worketh death. In the best and most healthy characters
the sense of sin means something very different: not that I
am going to be punished and must bear the physical or
social consequences of what I have done; but that I did
what I ought not to have done; that I was selfish, cowardly,
unready, untrue, and cruel; that I failed at the test and
that the failure was my own fault; that it has sent me at
a distance from God; that it has cost me in my character
the loss of liberty and spontaneousness; that it has produced in me a cowardly mistrust of myself in all moral effort; that it has given me a slavish fear of God in place
of the natural love and trust which His children enjoy. A
man who has such a conscience of his sins will not, in seeking forgiveness, be chiefly concerned about their physical
or social consequences. The fear of punishment will be
absorbed in, or at least be subordinate to, the nobler
anxiety as to how the ethical and religious disturbance produced in his nature by sin may be removed. For him forgiveness will mean reconciliation with God His Father;
the dissipation of the evil conscience which rises in him at
the presence of God; and the overcoming of that horrible
distrust of himself before temptation and before duty which
paralyses his will and renders him an easy prey to the
powers of evil. At the same time, looking to God as he
does, as God Almighty, of infinite grace and with command
of nature and of history as well as of the spiritual life of
man, he will not cease to pray for the reduction of even

82

the material consequences of his guilt. But he will not count the latter as the essence or even as the necessary result of his forgiveness. If he does he will be entertaining a conception of forgiveness which will only lead him away from, and blind his heart to, those moral results, by which alone God's pardon of us could be justified or were worth the taking by ourselves.

These truths, which are obvious to the higher instincts of our own nature, are plainly set before us in the Bible. Not without struggle and much passion; for it costs God's people, even under the special guidance of His Spirit which they enjoyed, no little argument, and even scepticism to reach them. The Revelation, of which the Bible is the record, encountered man upon every moral level upon which it has been given to the human heart to suffer and aspire. And therefore the account which the Old Testament contains of how men looked for and sought the Divine Pardon is very various. Yet it is one which steadily grows with Israel's increasing experience of God's manifestation of Himself and of His Providence in nature and history; throwing off by degrees every element of servile error and fear, till at last it becomes a noble and disinterested peace, in which a man learns to accept the spiritual elements of forgiveness for their own sake—the assurance of God's restored trust in him, the restoration of His communion, and the welcome burden of His will—and reckons as subordinate and incidental to these, such reliefs, as He may be pleased to send, of the outward afflictions which the sins have wrought.

At first—it was a necessary stage in their Divine education—the Hebrews appear to have had a very simple idea of the relations of sin, suffering, and forgiveness. In their language *the Lord brought down upon* a man's *head his own wickedness* (Judges 9:57); visited him with physical and other evils, and when He forgave him these were removed. The nation as a whole sinned, and in consequence suffered drought and famine, and when these did not avail to produce penitence in them, oppression, slaughter, and even exile at the hands of heathen powers regarded as the instruments of God's rightous anger against them. And His forgiveness was assured to their penitence when He delivered them from their enemies and restored to them their political freedom and the opportunity of worshipping Him in their own land. In all this there was a profound truth: the conviction, namely, that as God is One, so His world is one; that morality to use a modern phrase is "of the natural order of things"; and that the Divine Providence sways nature and history for the high ends of righteousness and grace.

Yet, as we can easily see, the effect of such simple views upon such an experience, was to create and foster the belief that physical and political disaster, whether it fell on the nation or on the individual, always implied the sinfulness of its victims, and that conversely prosperity always proved their righteousness. How strong and pervasive a dogma this became in Israel may be perceived not only from the quantity of the Old Testament prophecy directed against it, but from the bitter struggle and deep passion which it cost the prophets and psalmists to reach an opposite conviction. Both the nation as a whole and certain great souls in their private experience[1] found themselves in

---

[1]Such a Psalmist as the author of Psalm LXXIII; Jeremiah; and the author of the Book of Job.

world. They prayed that He would *make perfect that which concerned them*. And even within this life He often did so. But so far from imagining that forgiveness was coincident with the removal of the sufferings which their sins had brought upon them, they found that it gave them new strength and willingness to bear these, so long as it should please God to continue to afflict them. They accepted their pain; the power to do so was one of the results of forgiveness. Yet after this life was over they looked for one which should be full of blessedness and glory. *Nevertheless,* in spite of every suffering and every doubt it breeds, *I am with Thee: Thou hast holden my right hand. Thou shalt guide me with Thy counsel and afterward receive me to glory.*

In the New Testament we find the full results of this age-long struggle to light and peace. They are so simple that to describe them requires few words. Only we must first notice that our Lord found it necessary again to contradict the dogma (for it still lingered) that all suffering meant guilt (John 9:3). And again the inference was clear that the forgiveness of sins did not essentially consist in the removal of suffering. Although, in the divine power bestowed on Him, He sometimes healed the sinner when He forgave him, the forgiveness was granted before the healing. In His picture of the penitent prodigal, although the latter is received as a son as he was at the beginning and clothed with the robe and the ring, yet he himself had been satisfied, were it his father's will, to be taken back only as a hired servant. For his pure penitence rightly discerned that forgiveness was something essentially different from the full removal of the consequences of his sin. It is not otherwise with the Apostles, who in speaking of God's pardon emphasise the ethical and religious results.

86

Only, and still more brightly and confidently than with the prophets, the New Testament assures those who are forgiven of their full blessedness and freedom in the glory of their Father hereafter. *They shall hunger no more, neither thirst any more . . . and God shall wipe away every tear from their eyes.*

The sum of the matter then is that we cannot say, God *never* remits to a forgiven man the consequences of his sins. He is the God and Father of our Lord and Saviour Jesus Christ who in His Name healed the paralytic at the same time that He said: *Son, thy sins be forgiven thee!* He is the omnipotent Creator who in His physical world has provided such wonderful means of healing, recuperation, and repair. But what we can affirm, both from Scripture and experience, is that such a remission does not always nor even generally occur when forgiveness itself has become sure. To go back for a moment to Scripture and to a most clear example there, we read of David who by God's grace found pardon, if ever man did, and who nevertheless in his kingdom, in his family and in his own person bore to the day of his death the punishment of the great crime of which he so nobly repented. And we all—or at least those of us who are past our youth—have known men and women who have as nobly repented of their sins as David, and who nevertheless in the unremitting pains of a long life have had to pay the heavy debts they incurred by the folly and recklessness of their youth. Did not Israel of old, although forgiven, *receive of the Lord's hand double for all her sins?*

In all which there is at once a great consolation and a terrible warning. A great consolation—for to those who are compassed with infirmities of their own making, irremovable on this side the grave, there comes the message that within these, and in spite of these, the peace of God may be found; that they may bear them not as convicts or guilty slaves, but as sons, and find in them not punishment but purification and the means of holding closer to the God of grace, than ever they had been able to do without them. And a terrible warning—Brothers, *be not deceived, God is not mocked. Whatsoever a man soweth, that shall he reap.* Sin, and you may be forgiven, but you shall never so long as life lasts be able to count on freedom from the consequences. Even within the moral sphere these may persist. Sin, and though God's love sweep away the hopelessness of the future, and God's Spirit put in you a new will and new courage, it shall be with heavier weights that you run your race, with increased temptations that you must battle up to the end of the day—temptations besides that you shall never encounter without the shame and weakness of having been yourself their guilty cause.

III

In what then does the forgiveness of sin essentially consist? In the infinite riches of God's grace by Christ Jesus, it consists in many spiritual results, of which I have already, from Scripture and our experience, quoted several. But among these there is one to which we may devote the rest of this sermon for three reasons, because it is ethically the most inspiring, because it is that on which Scripture appears to lay most stress, and because, at the same time, it is one so often overlooked by ourselves.

From at least the time of the prophets up to the end of the New Testament the element in Forgiveness which the

Bible most frequently emphasises is God's new trust in the soul He has pardoned: the faith that despite our frailty, our unworthiness, our guilt; despite the mistrust and despair which the memory of our sin induces, God still trusts us, God believes us capable of doing better, God confides to us the interests and responsibilities of His work on earth. That according to the Bible is the ethical meaning of forgiveness—God's belief in us, God's hope for us, God's will to work with us, God's trust to us of services and posts in His kingdom.

So long ago Isaiah found it: when immediately after his guilt had been removed by a sacrament of fire, he felt himself receive—not, mark you, to begin with a definite commission to God's people, but the opportunity, upon his own will and motive, to give himself to the message and work which God proclaimed as open. He had called himself *a man of unclean lips, and dwelling in the midst of an unclean people.* But when his iniquity was taken away and his sin purged; and he heard the voice of the Lord saying *Whom shall I send and who will go for us?*—he himself in the great consciousness of freedom which forgiveness brought, and in the full enjoyment of God's restored trust in him, cried out: *Here am I, send me!* And at once he received his commission.

So also long ago a Psalmist felt it—the Psalmist who, more than any other, declares to us the purely ethical motives that drive men to pray for Pardon. Forgiveness came to him, too, as the instinct of a great commission from God, who trusted him.

Deliver me from blood guiltiness, O God of my salvation, And my tongue shall sing aloud of thy rightousness. O Lord, open thou my lips, And my mouth shall show forth

89

thy praise. I will teach transgressors thy ways, And sinners shall be converted unto thee (Psalm 51:13, 14).

So long ago another prophet saw it when he made God's trust of men the starting point of all salvation and providence. *For He said: Surely they are my people: children who cannot lie* or prove false. They did lie, they did fail: all the time they proved rebels to His will and traitors to the trust that He reposed in them. But He forgave them by trusting them again. He said *they are children that will not lie: so He became their saviour. In all their affliction He was afflicted, and the Angel of His Presence saved them. In His love and in His pity He redeemed them; and He bare them and carried them all the days of old* (Isaiah 63:8, 9). The whole glorious history of their salvation and their long sustenance started from their God's gracious trust in their unworthy and tainted souls.

In the New Testament it is not otherwise. Our Lord's announcements of pardon are sometimes followed by the words: *Go and sin no more.* They are in the imperative mood, but it is the fashion of the grammar of the day. What they mean is—Thou wilt sin no more: I have confidence in thee! When Peter fell by denying His Lord at the critical hour, the assurance of forgiveness came to his heartfelt penitence in the gift of a new commission in His Lord's service. *Simon, son of Jonas, lovest thou me? He saith unto him, Yea, Lord, thou knowest that I love thee. Jesus saith unto him: Feed my lambs,* and again *Tend my sheep,* and again *Feed my sheep.*

Such, then, is the Biblical doctrine of forgiveness. Amid the many blessings in which through the infinite riches of His mercy in Christ, it consists, this stands out, the most wonderful and inspiring essential of all: that God Himself should trust us when we have lost all trust of ourselves: should believe us capable of standing when we have fallen, of overcoming where we have only known defeat; and of again doing the work, in which we have been so lax and unfaithful.

For it is just in all this that the tremendous moral possibilities of forgiveness consist. Let a man merely off the consequences of his sin and by that alone you do not give him much more than room and time to grow better: *though the goodness of God also leadeth to repentance,* and if men's hearts were only more open to the respites and reliefs of His ordinary Providence, they would find in them all the grace, which they are too apt to associate only with the crises of worship and religious feeling. Tell a man in addition that God so loved him that He gave His Son to die for him, and when the man believes it, though his heart was dry and obdurate, you shall indeed have wakened all over his experience—as I dare say nothing else ever did wake in human nature—the springs of wonder, gratitude and hope. But you cannot make him feel the depths of that love, you cannot carry his gratitude or his hope to their fullest pitch, you cannot add to his affections a new conscience or fortify them past every shock, till you tell him that God's love for him includes God's trust in his loyalty, in his power to make a new start, to stand firm, and, though he should be the most fallen and stunted of men, in his power to grow at last to the full stature of his manhood. Without this trust of God forgiveness is only indulgence and the experience of it becomes a mere escape. But with the sense of being trusted forgiveness becomes a conscience, and puts into a man a new sense of honour to do his best and his bravest for the God who believes in him.

many have immediately been changed and shall be to the end of time; but I do know that in the sense of forgiveness, which I have put before you, you will expand the sensations of an hour to the experience of a lifetime and make God's forgiveness of you as wide and as constant as His common Providence.

IV

I said at the outset that we would confine ourselves to the question: In what does the Forgiveness of Sins consist? and would not take up the other equally important one, How is the Forgiveness of Sin procured and assured to us? But as Christians we can never forget the answer to this other, for it is the central fact of our religion: through the love of God, who gave His own Son to die for us on the Cross. And I now conclude, with the bearing of this fact on a further application of the truth we have been studying together.

As it was Christ who brought God's pardon to us, let us remember that God's great trust, so manifest in it, is continued to us so far as we hold to Christ and abide in Him. Apart from the grace, that is so richly every man's in Christ, God cannot trust us nor could we presume on the assurance of our forgiveness nor prove ourselves worthy of it. Therefore, in this most liberating of all ethical experiences do not let a man ever feel himself independent. But as day by day the goodness of God comes upon him; as he wakens every morning into the wonder of God's patience with his unworthy soul; as the great occasions of life come upon him, work, influence, friendship, love; as knowledge, and progress and a stable character become sure to him—

93

let him remember that these are not given to him for his own sake, but for Christ's. Let him say to himself: I am trusted with them all by God, and assured of them all, only in so far as I live in Christ and by the grace which He bestows.

❦

Forgive Us Our Trespasses *

J. WALLACE HAMILTON

"... *his father saw him, and had compassion, and ran, and fell on his neck, and kissed him.*— Luke 15:20

A TYPICALLY MODERN woman wrote a verse that found its way into the columns of a daily newspaper;

I wish there were some one
Who would hear confession.
Not a priest—I do not want to be told of my sins;
Not a mother—I do not want to give sorrow;
Not a friend—she would not know enough;
Not a lover—he would be too partial;
Not a God—He is far away;
But some one who would be friend, lover, mother, priest,
     God, all in one,
And a stranger besides—who would not condemn or
     interfere;

---

*From *Horns and Halos* by J. Wallace Hamilton, copyright 1954 by Fleming H. Revell Company. Used by permission.

Who, when everything is said from beginning to end,
Would show the reason of it all
And tell you to go ahead
And work it out your own way.

> Jeanne D'Orge,
> in *N. Y. Times Book Review.*

"I have sinned," the prodigal said to his father. "I have sinned." And in the heart of every human there is something that understands him. God has given every human soul a sense of guilt, a vague, uneasy restlessness, and it is one of our most precious possessions. It is the proof of our sonship. It is the call of Eternity. It is God's unbroken hold upon our hearts. What a pity we have gone to the shallows about the meaning of that! At no point has the secular view of life proved more bankrupt than in its incapacity to understand and effectively deal with the reality of human sin. Jauntily it has dismissed sin as irrelevant and turned from the great depths, the profound wisdom of the Hebrew prophets, the realism of Shakespeare and the great dramatists and the message of redemption in the New Testament to the unbelievably shallow philosophy of Rousseau about the goodness of man and his ability to save himself without God.

Meanwhile, the sin of man has piled up in tragic consequence. It has not helped much to call it error, absence of good, false concept of mind—as though, by waving a metaphysical wand, we could banish jails, wars, concentration camps. Something is here, something, filling life with tragic consequence, and if it isn't real it might as well be. Neither has it helped much to call sin by other names, by the soft names that take responsibility out of action. We've had our share of that, too. If you get a broken home, it isn't anything that anybody is responsible for. It is incompatibility, or some other word the lawyer supplies at fifty dollars a dozen.

> In olden days when people heard
> Some swindler huge had come to grief,
> They used a good old Saxon word,
> And called the man a thief;
> But language such as that today,
> Upon man's tender feeling grates,
> So they look wise, and simply say,
> He re-hy-poth-e-cates.

New labels for old evils. But changing the name of them doesn't remove them nor lessen their consequences in life. Someone said that when the prodigal son fretted at home, wanting to be away, he called what he was doing "independence." That was such a nice name. Out in the far country with bright eyes looking into his, he called it "pleasure." When he lost his money, he called it "bad luck." When he got down to feeding the pigs, he called himself a fool. But when he thought straight about it, he said, "Father, I have sinned." That is authentic.

Let us look again at what the Gospel calls "forgiveness." "I believe in the forgiveness of sin." People have been saying that in the stately creed, for sixteen hundred years. What do we mean by it? Jesus said, "When you pray, Say . . . forgive us our trespasses." What do we mean by the forgiveness of sin?

First of all, it is a *pardon*. We must begin with that—

96

forgiveness is a pardon, a fresh start, another chance, a new beginning. It is the lifting of a burden, the canceling of a debt, God's answer to the cry of a tortured conscience. "Have mercy, O God, according to thy loving kindness, according to the multitude of thy tender mercies blot out my transgressions."

Into the study of a minister came a big, handsome six-foot fellow with all his flags flying at half-mast. In the language of the athletic field, he told his story: "I've been benched for a foul play. Is there a chance for me, or must I sit out the rest of life's game on the side lines?" The minister sat there, listening to a sordid story involving the spoilation of other lives. "How old are you? What quarter of the game is it?" "The first," said the boy. "And that means there are still three quarters of the game to play?" "Yes, sir, three quarters." "And you really want to get back into the game?" "Yes, sir, if the coach will let me." "All right, son, let's get down on our knees here and ask Him." And the great miracle came again, there in the stillness, with no altar but a chair, no ritual but a man making a clean breast of his sins; and then the gladness of heart, the banishment of fear, the release of the pent-up soul in the pardon, in the forgiveness of sin. That is practical enough!

If I were a psychiatrist, I should hardly call it wisdom to ignore this most potent of all relief procedures. Blessed is the man, happy is the man, whose transgression is forgiven, whose sin is covered, in whose heart there is no guilt. Dr. A. J. Cronin was a physician in England until his health broke, and then he became an author. He told the story of a young nurse in charge of a little boy brought to the hospital of which he was the head. The boy was desperately ill with diphtheria; his throat was choked with membrane, and he had only a slender chance to live. A tube was inserted to give him breath, but as the nurse sat by the cot she dozed off, went to sleep, and awakened to find that the tube had become blocked. Instead of following instructions, clearing the tube of membrane—a matter of nursing routine—she lost her head and committed the unpardonable sin of bolting in panic. Hysterically she called the doctor out of sleep, but when he got there the child was dead.

He was angry beyond all power of expression that a child should die so needlessly, by such blundering, inexcusable negligence. Of course she was through; her career was finished. That same night he dipped his pen in vitriol, wrote his report to the health board demanding her immediate expulsion and called her in and read it with voice trembling with resentment. She stood there in pitiful silence, a thin, gawky Welsh girl, half fainting with shame and remorse. "Well, have you nothing to say for yourself?" More silence, and then a stammering plea. "Give me . . . give me another chance."

The doctor was taken aback. Certainly he had no thought of that; it was a breach of discipline, and there was nothing to do but punish her. He dismissed her, sealed his report and went to bed. That night he couldn't sleep. A queer echo of a far-off Word came floating in, kept whispering, "Forgive us our trespasses . . ."

Next morning he went to his desk and tore up the report. Then he went on to tell how this slim, nervous girl became the head of a large hospital and one of the most honored nurses in England. Pardon—another chance—a fresh start:—certainly forgiveness means that. The writers of the New Testament leap to their feet and cup their hands

to their lips to shout it; fairly bankrupt human speech trying to express it. Good news: there is forgiveness with
God! There is a land of beginning again.

> There is a fountain filled with blood,
>> Drawn from Immanuel's veins;
> And sinners, plunged beneath that flood,
>> Lose all their guilty stains.

Forgiveness—it is the word that rings like music all
through the New Testament. It was the impulse in which
the Church was born. It was what the early Christians
preached about as they went into the fear-haunted, fatal-
istic, pessimistic Greek world. "Fatalism is a lie," they said,
"God gives us another chance." Of course the Greeks
laughed at it. To them it was foolishness. Celsus, the Greek
philosopher, heaped scorn on their shabby movement.
"Every other teacher," he said, "summons to him the best
people, the clever and the good, but this crazy Jesus calls
to him the beaten and the broken, the ragtag and the bob-
tail, the failures and the scum." But far from being shamed
by that, the Church gloried in it. "Yes, it's true," they said,
"Christ does take the broken and defeated, but He doesn't
leave them broken and defeated. Out of the failures you
would throw away He makes new men; He gives them
another chance." Our word "Gospel" means "good news,"
and this is good news: "Now we have redemption through
his blood, even the forgiveness of sin."

But now we must go deeper. Forgiveness that stops
with pardon, ignoring the profound, ethical demand involved in pardon, is more immoral than sin. To give a man
a new chance without a new heart, to forgive evil without

99

destroying it, to let men off without lifting them up is to demoralize their souls; it encourages them to sin with impunity, and thus make even the grace of God an accomplice of continued evil. Protestants sometimes accuse Roman Catholicism of this. "What's the good of it?" they say. "A man sins, goes to confession, gets absolution, then goes out to sin again because forgiveness has come too cheaply." Of course the Catholics resent the accusation, and I believe rightly so, because it is neither fair nor true to say that the Roman Catholic Church encourages evil. It serves, however, to illustrate a sub-Christian view of forgiveness all too common in Christian history, Protestant and Catholic alike—the disposition to think of forgiveness in terms of safety, protection—to let men off from the consequence of sin without saving them from the sin. It is like the man who was asked by the judge if he had anything to say before sentence was pronounced; the man said it was always his policy to let by-gones be by-gones, and so far as he was concerned, he was willing to drop the whole matter right there. You had better not let men off unless you lift them up!

Two major theories of forgiveness have come down the stream of Christian history, symbolized by two worthy professions—the law and medicine. The lawyer thinks in legal terms and speaks in legal language; God to him is the great Judge and man is a prisoner before the bar of Divine justice, having broken God's law. Christ stands as "attorney for the defense," pleading the sinner's case, canceling his debt, getting the sinner off from the penalty of his transgression. In the language of the court room, he interprets the forgiveness of God. This legal concept has dominated the thinking of theology, or at least the theology of

55467

the Western Church, of which we are the offspring. When the Apostle Paul, who was the link between the Hebrew and the Gentile world, entered the cities of the Roman Empire, he translated Christianity from Hebrew into Roman patterns of thought; his language is legal language, his illustrations are legal illustrations, because the Roman mind was a legal mind and thought about everything in terms of law and government. The argument of the Epistle to the Romans is one of justifications by faith—of how God can be just and the justifier of the unjust; it it all legal phraseology.

Then, as the centuries passed and the Roman Church took up the doctrine of forgiveness, it devised an elaborate sacramental system, built around the idea of rewards, penalties, penance, purgatory, confession and pardon, until the great reality was almost lost in the ecclesiastical machinery designed to promote it.

Despite the Reformation, we have largely inherited that legal notion of forgiveness. It is still in our minds to think of it mainly as a means of escape from the consequence of transgression. I am not proposing that we scrap the vocabulary of the law court. What we need most to do, Catholic and Protestant alike, is to get back behind the vocabulary and the machinery to the reality they were originally meant to express. What we need Christ for is not to save us from the punishment of sin but to save us from the sin. That is why, in my judgment, the doctor's mind comes nearer the reality of the New Testament. The doctor thinks not in terms of law but in terms of life. Sin to him is like a disease, destroying life. Forgiveness is the cure of sin, the infusion of a new life to drive the evil out and to restore health and wholeness. Read through the

101

Gospels and, with the exception of a parable or two, you will wonder how anyone could ever have thought of forgiveness as a legal transaction. Jesus went about curing people. He paid no attention to the sacrificial system of the Temple. He got Himself nicknamed "the great Physician."

And where healing of the body ends and the soul begins, who can say? To some people sick in body, He said, "Thy sins are forgiven thee," anticipating by two thousand years that modern psychotherapy which knows well that much of our body sickness is rooted in deeper ailments of the soul. What Jesus was attempting in every case was cure; He seemed to pay no attention to the legal notion. Indeed, he often had to clash with legal minds to work His cure. They brought before Him a woman, taken in sin. "The law says she deserves stoning. What say you?" He didn't answer. Stooping down, He wrote on the ground. When He looked up they were gone; no one was there but the woman. "Where are those thine accusers? Hath no man condemned thee?" "No man, Lord." "Neither do I condemn thee: go and sin no more." You see, they were out to save the law, and He was out to save a life. He came not to condemn, He said, but to save.

But suppose we go deeper still. There is a profound social demand in forgiveness. Forgiveness is *pardon,* and it is personal cure; it is also a process of life and the Christian weapon of social redemption. There is a story of King Albert of Belgium when, in the First World War, as the Germans ravished their little country, the Belgians were bitter and bowed down with sorrow. A small group of children, with their teacher, gathered at a roadside shrine outside the village, kneeling to pray to the Virgin. They

102

were saying the Lord's Prayer; they came to the words, "Forgive us our trespasses as we . . . ," and stopped, choked, and couldn't go on. They were thinking of their country. "But we must say it," the Sister told them, and she went on, "Forgive us our trespasses as we . . . ;" she stopped again; another voice took up the words, "As we forgive those who trespass against us." It was their King; he stood behind their kneeling figures with bowed head and burdened heart. I don't see how we can miss this social note of forgiveness. There are sixty-two words for forgiveness in the New Testament, and twenty-two times it means forgiveness for others. Without that, there is no forgiveness for ourselves.

The one character Jesus pictured as the most impossible to respect is in His parable of the unmerciful slave. You must allow for a bit of humor in this story, and for a twinkle in His eye, as Jesus deliberately exaggerated the details, for no slave in Palestine could owe ten thousand talents, (ten million dollars, someone estimates it) which was more than ten times the total taxes of the country! The slave owed a debt he couldn't pay, not in his whole lifetime and, begging on his knees for mercy, he was forgiven the debt. Then, with all that mercy shown him, he goes straight from his knees to wring the neck of the poor devil who owed him twenty dollars!

Jesus told the story to show that people are not forgiven who are not forgiving; that they have no kinship with the Father unless they possess the Father's spirit; that all of God's forgiveness is wasted on us unless we are moved by His mercy to be merciful. There was nothing legal in His thought about it; *if you don't forgive, God won't.* He was thinking of the corrosion in the human soul that harbors hate and resentment toward another, and how impossible it is for God's grace to live in a soul that is graceless.

Peter had wanted to keep it legal and statistical: "Lord, how often, how often shall my brother sin against me and I forgive him? Seven times?" He knew he had better put it more than three times, which was the customary allowance of the law. He knew he had to be generous with Jesus. "Seven times?" And Jesus said, "Peter, there is no limit to forgiveness. Not seven times, but four hundred and ninety times seventy times seven." In other words, forgiveness is not an act. It is an attitude; it is not a spurt but a spirit. You can't forgive four hundred and ninety times without getting the habit.

Here, then, is the Christian weapon against social evil. We are to go out into the world, we who have been forgiven a debt we could never pay; we are to go armed with the spirit of forgiveness, heal the hurts, right the wrongs and change society with forgiveness. Of course, it isn't practical. Any realist knows that. Life is a matter of—getting even, saving face, being ready to lick all comers—an eye for an eye, a tooth for a tooth. You mean we are to do good to those who hurt us, and after all the vile things our enemies do to us, forgive them? You're crazy. Maybe in some other world, but this is no world to get soft in.

Well, we have been following the practical way for a long time now, and at least we ought to be humble about it and be clear about what this means. The heart of the question is how to get rid of our enemies, or how to get rid of the bitterness that *makes* enemies. Get that straight and at least you will avoid some of the sentimental caricatures of forgiveness and false application of its spirit. Soft-heartedness is not forgiveness. Soft-heartedness does not get rid of enemies. It feeds them, fattens them, appeases them, and it makes the good in you an accomplice of the wrong in them.

Nor does what is commonly called "non-resistance to evil" get rid of your enemies. How could any one, knowing Jesus, equate the forgiveness He taught with negative non-resistance? No one has ever resisted evil as courageously as He. Principal Jacks said, "One of my teachers in college tried to make a better Christian of me by persuading me to adopt the principle of non-resistance to evil. I was moved to tell him that if he ever detected me in doing evil and failed to resist me to the utmost of his power, using force if necessary, that he was no friend of mine but an enemy of God and a man whom I would denounce at first opportunity." God resists evil. The Cross on the hill outside Jerusalem is the unfathomable measure of His resistance.

The question is—How? How to resist it, cure it, destroy it? One old fellow, interviewed on the radio, said, "I'll be ninety years old tomorrow, and I haven't an enemy in the world." The announcer said, "That's a happy thought." "Yep," the old fellow went on, "I've outlived them all." It's a good trick if you can do it. Narvaez, the Spanish patriot, lay dying, and his Father Confessor asked him if he had forgiven all his enemies. "Father," he smiled, "I have no enemies. I have shot them all." That's an idea too! The Christian technique of forgiveness is to get rid of enemies by getting rid of enmity. In all His teachings about loving your enemies, turning the other cheek and doing good to those who hurt you, Jesus is talking about a wholesome, common sense way of getting along with people, of curing evil at its source and getting rid of the bitterness that sets men against men and nation against nation. The easiest way to do anything is to do it the easiest way, which seems ridiculously obvious but almost impossible for human nature to learn. We have never been big enough to try the obvious so we laugh at it, call it "idealism" and talk it down. But it makes pretty good sense when it gets out of a book into someone's life. Lincoln did it, and because he did it, he holds our hearts in a hush. At the height of the Civil War, when feeling was bitterest, at a White House reception he dropped a kindly remark about the South, and a woman there flared up, shocked that he could speak kindly of his enemies when he should want to destroy them. Lincoln looked at her and said slowly, "Madam, do I not destroy my enemies when I make them my friends?"

Now, we are not skilled in this technique at all. We have had so little experience in it, even in personal relationships that, collectively confronted with this enormous mass of enmity, bitterness, impenitent brutality, we are profoundly afraid to even risk it. But now we have come to the place where it is a case of "forgive—or else!" These multiplying hatreds can destroy us. This chain reaction of evil —hate breeding hate, wars making more wars, violence begetting violence, eye for eye, tooth for tooth—must be broken. We know, deep in our hearts, that it is no good. We shout loudly about being strong because we fear our weakness, and we build dreadnaughts because our souls are filled with dread.

Bishop Hazen Werner told me recently of a man whose son was among the first to be sent to the Pacific. "Getting on the train at the end of his last leave, there were so many things I should have said and didn't. Now he's going

106

away and I may not see him again. If he's killed, I hope every Jap will die. *What am I saying?* I can't even think that and be Christian. When he left, I got into my car and drove off into the country, and it kept coming back— 'If he dies, I hope every Jap will die.' Forgive me, Lord, for the thought. I fought it. I mastered it. And then a year later, there was the reality. We lost him, but I was ready. I had faced it. We're taking his insurance money and we're putting it into missions for Japan; for what Japan needs, and what we all need, is not more punishment but redemption."

Darkness cannot drive out darkness; only light can do that. More ignorance cannot drive out ignorance; only knowledge can do that. More evil cannot drive out evil; only goodness can do that. Better start with this somewhere tomorrow:

"Father, forgive us ours . . . as we forgive theirs."

From Hostility to Love

※ ※ ※

If there is one thing that every member of a congregation needs, it is love. There are no exceptions—rich and poor, old and young, wise and simple, doctor, lawyer, merchant, chief—all need to love and be loved. Just as fresh air, nourishment, and rest are necessary for physical health, so love, understanding, and acceptance are necessary for emotional and spiritual health.

This is a predominant emphasis in contemporary psychology and psychotherapy. Psychiatrists such as Dr. Menninger have said, "Our mental health depends on our capacity to love."[1] Dr. Rollo May expressed a similar thought when he said, "To be capable of giving and receiving mature love is as sound a criterion as we have for the fulfilled personality."[2]

What psychologists as saying, based on extensive research and clinical findings, ministers and theologians have been saying for centuries. Love is one of the central themes of the New Testament. The first commandment according to Jesus was to love God. The second was to love one's neighbor. Paul said, "The whole law is fulfilled in one word, 'You shall love your neighbor as yourself'" (Gal. 5:14). Over and over

---

[1]William Menninger, "Tensions in Family Life." *Pastoral Psychology,* Vol. IV, No. 33 (April 19, 1953), p. 18.

[2]May, *Man's Search for Himself* (New York: W. W. Norton & Company, Inc., 1953), p. 238.

this thought occurs. Love is listed as the greatest of all values. "So faith, hope, love abide, these three; but the greatest of these is love" (1 Cor. 13:13).

When the pastor is speaking on love, he has the assurance that he is dealing with man's deepest emotional need. Without love life is incomplete. No member of his congregation is so successful that he does not need love, for success has little value unless it is shared. There is no one so rich that he does not need love, for nothing can be purchased that is a substitute for love. There is no one so wise that his wisdom replaces his need for love, for without love knowledge becomes a mere accumulation of information. There is no one so famous, so well known that he does not need love, for fame and popularity become hollow and empty unless one feels accepted and loved.

However, although Jesus, the writers of the New Testament, psychologists and psychiatrists, preachers and theologians all speak of love as one of man's deepest needs, the world is still filled with hostility. There will be some in the congregation who have been deprived of love; there will be some who frankly doubt its value; there will be some who desperately want to love but don't know how; there will be some who find it hard to love. Their lives are characterized by jealousy and bitterness rather than by love.

In family counseling, in pastoral care, and in church administration, the pastor will have many opportunities to help people overcome their hostile feelings. Each one is different. Each one must be understood in the light of his own background. All the skill, the patience, and the understanding that a pastor possesses are required. But whenever he helps a person drain off his negative, hostile, bitter feelings and replace them with attitudes of love and understanding, he is performing a reconciling, redemptive task. Nothing is more needed.

109

Hostility hurts the one who hates and the one who is hated.
Love helps the one who is loved and the one who loves.

Hostility destroys.
Love builds.

Hostility produces suffering and pain.
Love produces health and wholeness.

Hostility rejects.
Love accepts.

Hostility separates, estranges.
Love unites, joins.

Hostility is vindictive.
Love is magnanimous.

Hostility is revengeful.
Love is forgiving.

Hostility is resentful.
Love is understanding, helpful.

Hostility stresses the faults and the flaws.
Love stresses one's good points and continues in spite of
the flaws.

Hostility hopes for the worst.
Love expects the best.

Hostility separates men from God.
Love opens the way for God.

Some hostility is so deep-rooted it must be handled by a
specialist, one who can help the parishioner understand the
source and cause of his bitterness. There are many who can
be helped only on an individual basis, in a counseling relationship in which they can discover their own feelings and
understand their own behavior as well as that of others.

110

All can be helped by good preaching on the subject of love. This is all that some people need. Their lives may be changed by effective preaching that stresses the love of God and man.

(1) Through preaching the pastor can interpret the biblical teachings on the nature and power of love. Anything that is stressed so repeatedly in the Bible cannot be ignored. "A new commandment I give to you, that you love one another . . ." (John 13:34).

(2) Through preaching the pastor can make clear the findings and evidence of the psychological sciences concerning the deep significance of love. This does not mean he uses psychological terms in his sermons or that he lectures instead of preaches. Ours is a psychological age. Psychology has much to say about human behavior. This is one place where psychology and the New Testament agree.

(3) Through preaching the pastor can keep alive in the minds of his people the goal of achieving better interpersonal relations. It is a process—it is never complete, but everyone should be growing in his capacity to understand, accept, forgive, and love. When the pastor presents this ideal in preaching, he is free to listen in counseling.

(4) Through preaching the pastor can make practical applications of obeying the law of love in the home, between parent and child, on the job, in the church, and in the world at large.

(5) Through preaching the pastor can help people to understand others, to be aware of the needs of others, to be sensitive to their feelings, to be willing to forgive their mistakes—and thus to love.

(6) Through preaching the pastor can preach the glad, good news that "God is love," that everyone is loved by God and thus can love others. "We love, because he first loved us" (1 John 4:19).

111

❧

The New Commandment of
Love to One Another*

FREDERICK W. ROBERTSON

"A new commandment I give unto you, that ye love one another; as I have loved you, that ye also love one another."—John 13:34

THESE WORDS derive impressiveness from having been spoken immediately before the last Supper, and on the eve of the great Sacrifice: the commandment of Love issued appropriately at the time of the Feast of Love, and not long before the great Act of Love. For the love of Christ was no fine *saying*: it cost Him His life to say these words with meaning, "As I have loved you."

There is a difficulty in the attempt to grasp the meaning of this command, arising from the fact that words change their meaning. Our Lord affixed a new significance to the word Love. It had been in use, of course, before, but the new sense in which He used it made it a new word.

His law is not adequately represented by the word Love; because love is, by conventional usage, appropriated to one species of human affection, which, in the commoner men, is the most selfish of all our feelings; in the best, too exclusive and individual to represent that charity which is universal.

---

*From *Sermons* by Frederick W. Robertson, Vol. I, copyright 1869, Fields, Osgood, and Company.

Nor is charity a perfect symbol of his meaning; for charity by use is identified with another form of love, which is but a portion of it,—almsgiving; and too saturated with that meaning to be entirely disengaged from it, even when we use it most accurately.

Benevolence or philanthropy, in derivation, come nearer to the idea: but yet you feel at once that these words fall short; they are too tame and cool; too merely passive, as states of feeling rather than forms of life.

We have no sufficient word. There is, therefore, no help for it, but patiently to strive to master the meaning of this mighty word Love, in the only light that is left us, the light of the Saviour's life: "As I have loved you;" that alone expounds it.

We will dispossess our minds of all preconceived notions; remove all low associations, all partial and conventional ones. If we would understand this law, it must be ever a "new" commandment, ever receiving fresh light and meaning from His life.

Take, I. The novelty of the law—"That ye love one another."

II. The spirit or measure of it—"As I have loved you."

I. Its novelty, A "new commandment:" yet that law was old. See 1 John 2:7, 8.

1. It was new as a historical fact. We talk of the apostolic mission as a matter of course; we say that the apostles were ordered to go and plant churches, and so we dismiss the great fact. But we forget that the command was rather

113

the result of a spirit working from within, than of an injunction working from without. That spirit was Love.

And when that new spirit was in the world, see how straightway it created a new thing. Men before that had travelled into foreign countries: the naturalist, to collect specimens; the historian, to accumulate facts; the philosopher, to hive up wisdom, or else he had stayed in his cell or grove to paint *pictures* of beautiful love. But the spectacle of an Apostle Paul crossing oceans, not to conquer kingdoms, nor to hive up knowledge, but to impart life,—not to accumulate stores for self, but to give, and to spend himself,—was new in the history of the world. The celestial fire had touched the hearts of men, and their hearts flamed; and it caught, and spread, and would not stop. On they went, that glorious band of brothers, in their strange enterprise, over oceans, and through forests, penetrating into the dungeon, and to the throne; to the hut of the savage feeding on human flesh, and to the shore lined with the skin-clad inhabitants of these far Isles of Britain. Read the account given by Tertullian of the marvellous rapidity with which the Christians increased and swarmed, and you are reminded of one of those vast armies of ants which move across a country in irresistible myriads, drowned by thousands in rivers, cut off by fire, consumed by man and beast, and yet fresh hordes succeeding interminably to supply their place.

A new voice was heard; a new yearning upon earth; man pining at being severed from his brother, and longing to burst the false distinctions which had kept the best hearts from each other so long; an infant cry of life—the cry of the young Church of God. And all this from Judea—

114

the narrowest, most bigoted, most intolerant nation on the face of the earth.

Now, I say that this was historically a new thing.

2. It was new in extent. It was, in literal words, an old commandment, given before both to Jew and Gentile. To the Jew; as, for instance, in Lev. 19:18. To the Gentile, in the recognition which was so often made of the beauty of the law in its partial application, as in the case of friendship, patriotism, domestic attachment, and so on.

But the difference lay in the extent in which these words "one another" were understood. By them, or rather by "neighbor," the Jew meant his countryman; and narrowed that down again to his friends among his countrymen; so that the well-known Rabbinical gloss upon these words, current in the days of Christ, was, "Thou shalt love thy neighbor, and hate thine enemy." And what the Gentile understood by the extent of the law of love, we may learn from the well-known words of their best and wisest, who thanked heaven that he was born a man, and not a brute; a Greek, and not a barbarian; as if to be a barbarian were identical with being a brute.

Now, listen to Christ's exposition of the word neighbor. "Ye have heard that it was said, Thou shalt love thy neighbor, and hate thine enemy. But I say unto you, Love your enemies." And He went further. As a specimen of a neighbor he specially selected one of that nation whom, as a theologian and a patriot, every Jew had been taught to hate. And just as the application of electricity to the innumerable wants of human life, and to new ends, is reckoned a new discovery and invention of modern times (though the fact has been familiar for ages to the Indian child in the forest of the far west, and applied by him for

115

ages to his childish sports), so the extension of this grand principle of love to all the possible cases of life, and to all possible persons,—even though the principle was known and applied long before, in love to friends, country, and relations,—is truly and properly a new commandment—a discovery, a gospel, a revelation.

3. It is new in being made the central principle of a system. Never had obedience before been trusted to a principle: it had always been hedged round by a law. The religion of Christ is not a law, but a spirit,—not a creed, but a life. To the one motive of love God has intrusted the whole work of winning the souls of His redeemed. The heart of man was made for love; pants and pines for it:— only in the love of Christ, and not in restrictions, can his soul expand. Now, it was reserved for One to pierce, with the glance of intuition, down into the springs of human action, and to proclaim the simplicity of its machinery. "Love," said the apostle after Him,—"Love is the fulfilling of the law."

We are told that in the new commandment the old perishes; that, under the law of love, man is free from the law of works. Let us see how.

Take any commandment,—for example, the sixth, the seventh, the eighth. I may abstain from murder and theft, deterred by law; because law has annexed to them certain penalties. But I may also rise into the spirit of Charity; then I am free from the law. The law was not made for a righteous man; the law no more binds or restrains me, now that I love my neighbor, than the dike built to keep in the sea at high tide restrains it when that sea has sunk to low-water mark.

116

Or the seventh. You may keep that law from dread of discovery,—or you may learn a higher Love: and then you *cannot* injure a human soul—you cannot degrade a human spirit. Charity has made the old commandment superfluous. In the strong language of St. John, you *cannot* sin, because you are born of God.

It was the proclamation of this, the great living principle of human obedience, not wth the pedantry of a philosopher, nor the exaggeration of an orator, but in the simple reality of life, which made this commandment of Christ a new commandment.

II. The spirit or measure of the law,—"as I have loved you."

Broadly, the love of Christ was the spirit of giving all he had to give. "Greater love hath no man than this, that a man lay down his life for his friend." Christ's love was not a sentiment; it was a self-giving. To that His adversaries bore testimony:—"He saved others; Himself He cannot save." Often as we have read these words, did it ever strike us,—and, if not, does it not bring a flash of surprise when we perceive it,—that these words, meant as taunt, were really the noblest panegyric, a higher testimony and more adequate far than even that of the centurion? "He saved others; Himself He cannot save." The first clause contained the answer to the second—"Himself He cannot save!" How *could* He, having saved others? How can any keep what he gives? How can any live for self, when he is living for others? Unconsciously, those enemies were enunciating the very principle of Christianity, the grand law of all existence, that only by losing self you can save

117

others; that only by giving life you can bless. Love gives itself. The mother spends herself in giving life to her child; the soldier, for his country; nay, even the artist produces nothing destined for immortality, nothing that will *live,* except so far as he has forgotten himself, and merged his very being in his work.

"He saved others; Himself He cannot save." That was the love of Christ. Now, to descend to particulars.

That spirit of self-giving manifests itself in the shape of considerate kindliness. Take three cases:—First, that in which He fed the people with bread. "I have compassion on the multitude, because they continue with me now three days, and have nothing to eat." There was a tenderness which, not absorbed in His own great designs, considered a number of small particulars of their state—imagined, provided; and this for the satisfaction of the lowest wants. Again, to the disciples: "Come ye yourselves apart into a desert place, and rest a while." He would not over-work them in the sublimest service. He did not grudge from duty their interval of relaxation; He even tenderly enforced it. Lastly, His dying words: "Behold thy mother! Woman, behold thy son!" Short sentences. He was too exhausted to say more. But in that hour of death-torture He could think of her desolate state when He was gone, and, with delicate, thoughtful attention, provide for her well-being.

There are people who would do great acts; but, because they wait for great opportunities, life passes, and the acts of love are not done at all. Observe, this considerateness of Christ was shown in little things. And such are the parts of human life. Opportunities for doing *greatly* seldom occur— life is made up of infinitesimals. If you compute the sum of happiness in any given day, you will find that it was composed of small attentions,—kind looks, which made the heart swell, and stirred into health that sour, rancid film of misanthropy, which is apt to coagulate on the stream of our inward life, as surely as we live in heart apart from our fellow-creatures. Doubtless, the memory of each one of us will furnish him with the picture of some member of a family whose very presence seemed to shed happiness: —a daughter, perhaps, whose light step even in the distance irradiated every one's countenance. What was the secret of such a one's power? What had she done? Absolutely nothing; but radiant smiles, beaming good humor, the tact of divining what every one felt and every one wanted, told that she had got out of self, and learned to think for others; so that at one time it showed itself in deprecating the quarrel, which lowering brows and raised tones already showed to be impending, by sweet words; at another, by smoothing an invalid's pillow; at another, by soothing a sobbing child; at another, by humoring and softening a father who had returned weary and ill-tempered from the irritating cares of business. None but she saw those things. None but a loving heart *could* see them.

That was the secret of her heavenly power. Call you those things homely trifles,—too homely for a sermon? By reference to the character of Christ, they rise into something quite sublime. For that is loving as He loved. And remark, too, these trifles prepare for larger deeds. The one who will be found in trial capable of great acts of love, is ever the one who is always doing considerate small ones. The soul which poured itself out to death upon the cross for the human race, was the spirit of Him who thought of the wants of the people, contrived for the rest of the disciples, and was thoughtful for a mother.

Once again:—It was a love never foiled by the unworthiness of those on whom it had been once bestowed. It was a love which faults, desertion, denial, unfaithfulness, could not chill, even though they wrung His heart. He had chosen; and He trusted. Even in ordinary manhood, that is a finely-tempered heart, one of no ordinary mould, which can say, "It ever was my way, and shall be still, when I do trust a man to trust him wholly." And yet there was everything to shake His trust in humanity. The Pharisees called him Good Master, and were circumventing him all the while. The people shouted hosannas, and three days afterwards were shrieking for his blood. One disciple who had dipped in the same dish, and been trusted with His inmost counsels, betrayed and deceived Him; another was ashamed of Him; three fell asleep while He was preparing for death, —all forsook Him. Yet nothing is more surprising than that unshaken, I had well-nigh said *obstinate,* trust with which He clung to His hopes of our nature, and believed in the face of demonstration.

As we mix in life, there comes, especially to sensitive natures, a temptation to distrust. In young life, we throw ourselves with unbounded and glorious confidence on such as we think well of,—an error soon corrected; for we soon find out—too soon—that men and women are not what they seem. Then comes disappointment; and the danger is a reaction of desolating and universal mistrust. For, if we look on the doings of man with a merely worldly eye, and pierce below the surface of character, we are apt to feel bitter scorn and disgust for our fellow-creatures. We have lived to see human hollowness; the ashes of the Dead Sea shores; the falseness of what seemed so fair; the mouldering

120

beneath the whited sepulchre: and no wonder if we are tempted to think "friendship *all* a cheat—smiles hypocrisy—words deceit;" and they who are what is called *knowing* in life contract, by degrees, as the result of their experience, a hollow distrust of men, and learn to sneer at apparently good motives. That demoniacal sneer which we have seen—ay, perhaps felt—curling the lip, at times, "Doth Job serve God for naught?"

The only preservative from this withering of the heart is Love. Love is its own perennial fount of strength. The strength of affection is a proof not of the worthiness of the object, but of the largeness of the soul which loves. Love descends, not ascends. The might of a river depends not on the quality of the soil through which it passes, but on the inexhaustibleness and depth of the spring from which it proceeds. The greater mind cleaves to the small with more force than the other to it. A parent loves the child more than the child the parent; and partly because the parent's heart is larger, not because the child is worthier. The Saviour loved His disciples infinitely more than His disciples Him, because His heart was infinitely larger. Love trusts on,—ever hopes and expects better things; and this, a trust springing from itself, and out of its own deeps alone.

And more than this. It is this *trusting* love that makes men what they are trusted to be, so realizing itself. Would you make men *trustworthy?* Trust them. Would you make them true? Believe them. This was the real force of that sublime battle-cry which no Englishman hears without emotion. When the crews of the fleet of Britain knew that they were *expected* to do their duty, they *did* their duty.

They felt in that spirit-stirring sentence that they were trusted: and the simultaneous cheer that rose from every ship was a forerunner of victory, the battle was half-won already. They went to serve a country which expected from them great things; and they *did* great things. Those pregnant words raised an enthusiasm for the chieftain who had thrown himself upon his men in trust, which a double line of hostile ships could not appall, nor decks drenched in blood extinguish.

And it is on this principle that Christ wins the hearts of His redeemed. He trusted the doubting Thomas; and Thomas arose with a faith worthy "of his Lord and his God." He would not suffer even the lie of Peter to shake his conviction that Peter might love Him yet; and Peter answered to that sublime forgiveness. His last prayer was extenuation and hope for the race who had rejected Him, and the kingdoms of the world are become His own. He has loved us, God knows why—I do not; and we, all unworthy though we be, respond faintly to that love, and try to be what He would have us.

Therefore, come what may, hold fast to love. Though men should rend your heart, let them not embitter or harden it. We win by tenderness; we conquer by forgiveness. O, strive to enter into something of that large celestial Charity which is meek, enduring, unretaliating, and which even the overbearing world cannot withstand forever. Learn the new commandment of the Son of God. Not to love, but to love as He loved. Go forth in this spirit to your life-duties; go forth, children of the Cross, to carry everything before you, and win victories for God by the conquering power of a love like His.

꩜

The Greatest of These *

HOWARD THURMAN

THERE ARE SOME PEOPLE who by temperament, by constitution, by glandular function seem to be naturally outgoing. A quality of spontaneity envelopes their personality and it reaches out and enfolds the other person. But for the most part, love is a discipline. A discipline! The discipline is rooted, as far as our personalities are concerned, in desire. There must be actively at work in the personality the desire to love, for this desire is the dynamic, the energy, the ceaseless rhythmic pulse that sustains the enterprise of the conscious mind. Again and again we discover, as we look at X or Y or Z, that the truth is we don't want to love him. We know that we ought to want to love him, but we don't want to. So we use a lot of phrases, such as: "I will love him for Christ's sake, but I don't like him."

This first basic step is very radical. I must want to love; I must desire *to desire* to love. Here I feel that the primary relationship of the individual with God is of the greatest importance and significance in the whole etiquette and morality and experience of love. I must offer to God my continuum of desires, expose them to the loving power of His spirit until at last there emerges in the very ground of the feeling tones of my life the focusing, the rallying, the

---

*From *The Growing Edge* by Howard Thurman. Copyright © 1956 by Howard Thurman. Reprinted by permission of Harper & Row, Publishers.

pointing of my desires in this regard. If I am to think and feel and experience love, I must search deep within me and relate myself to my God in whose Presence I expose all of me. When this is done, there does emerge in the body of my desires this special desire to love.

Now I am ready to get into my hands a tool that will enable me to implement my desires. Here the will comes in, the mind, the formal intensive processes of mind! I offer to my redirection, or my focused desires, the hard core of my decision. I now am able to make up my mind. And I now deliver to the dynamics of my personality the energy of will. There begins to emerge in me the will to love and the will to love becomes an organizing principle. It becomes a structuring principle, so that my desire *to desire* can be extended, implemented, developed. Where there is no will to love, the personality is unmanageable in this regard. The will to love has to be nourished, has to be fed, has to be related to an energy, or else it cannot be activated in the midst of all the vicissitudes of my living and my experiencing.

Once I have done this, there is another quality that I must put into the hands of my focused feeling tones, my focused desires, and that is another aspect of mind. For lack of a better term, I call it imagination. I must contrive some way by which I can dally with the other person. To use a colloquial term, I must "fool around" with the other person's personality. When my imagination is brought into play, as one of the additional tools for the implementation of my desiring, certain things begin to happen. I become able to project myself, first in little ways, into the other person's life, into the other person's situation. I am able to do that even as I remain myself.

124

A simple and dramatic illustration of this comes to my mind. I was visiting a friend of mine whose little boy had just learned to ride his kiddy cart. He rode it into the living room, and stopped at my feet and said, "Mr. Thurman, will you help me change my tire? I just had a blowout." I put my newspaper down. I helped him jack up the car. We took the old tire off and put the new one on. We put the jack back where it belonged. Then he sat in his car and tried to start the motor, but it didn't start. He pulled out the choke, then stepped on the starter; again nothing happened. He got out, lifted up one side of the hood and tinkered around. "Everything is all right here." He went around to the other side. "Everything is all right on this side." He got back into the car and stepped on the starter, but nothing happened. Then he began talking to his car, using language he had heard his father use under such circumstances. Still, nothing happened. Finally he said, "Maybe I don't have any gasoline." He got out, came over to me and said, "Do you have a pencil, Mr. Thurman?" I said, "Yes," and gave him a pencil. He took the top off the tank, put the pencil down into the tank, held it up and said, "Ah! The tank is empty." He returned the pencil. He went to the kitchen, got a glass of water from his mother, came back, sat down again in his kiddy cart, drank the water, started his motor and drove out of the living room into the kitchen.

There must be this sense of self-projection that enables me to move into the context in which the other person is living and look out on the common situation through the other person's eyes, even as I remain myself. When I do that, I make very important discoveries about this other person, discoveries which now inform my will and make it the major tool for the implementation of my desires. The use of imagination in this way gives me a sense of the right thing to say to precipitate the free flow of the good, healthy feeling that binds me to the other person and the other to me. I have begun to understand him, to know why he does the things he does.

Sometimes, simple mechanical devices can be resorted to as aids to understanding. A young couple in my church in San Francisco worked out a very simple device. Whenever the husband came home from work in the late afternoon, and was upset or irritable, he would leave his handkerchief dangling out of his jacket pocket. When his wife saw this, she knew that this was not a good day to do anything that was not just within the zones of harmonious agreement. On the other hand, if she had a certain apron that he had given her, he knew that this was not her day. Simple! We must study ways and means to release our desires that they may go home to their goals. It cannot be left to chance, it cannot be left to accident, it cannot be left to some kind of overbrooding sentimentality. It requires a discipline. The human spirit and personality must work at it . . . work at it . . . work at it. The will to love must not be damned up and blocked by things that could be removed if we took the time to think.

There is another service of imagination as a tool. It is illustrated in the Biblical record of a certain woman who was taken in adultery. The men who brought her to Jesus said, "Master, we caught this woman in the act of adultery. The law says she should be stoned to death. What do you say inasmuch as you declare that you came to fulfill the law, not to destroy it? What do you say? Do you ignore the law? What do you say?" And Jesus said, "Let the man among you who is without spot or blemish cast the first stone. After that, anybody may throw." And he wrote on the ground. After what seemed an eternity, I imagine, he lifted his face and looked at the woman. He had not looked at her before. He was a gentleman. He did not want his eyes to be mingled with the eyes of those who sat in judgment upon her. "Woman, where are they? Does no man condemn thee?"

"No, no, no . . ."

"Neither do I. Go, go into peace. And don't do it any more."

He met her where she was, admittedly an adulteress. He didn't slough that over. He met her where she was, but he treated her there, where she was, as if she were where she should have been. By so doing, he lifted her into the fulfillment of her personality.

I can love only when I meet you where you are, as you are, and treat you there as if you were where you ought to be. I see you where you are, striving and struggling, and in the light of the highest possibility of your personality, I deal with you there. My own religious faith is insistent that this can be done only out of a life of devotion. I must cultivate the inner spiritual resources of my life to such a point that I can bring you to my sanctuary, before His Presence, until, at last, I do not know you from myself. The discipline of the heart and the mind and the desire may become a lung through which God breathes. Therefore, if I say I love God and don't love you—I lie. If I say I love you and don't love God—I lie.

Now abideth faith, hope, and love. The greatest of these is *love*.

From Restlessness to Peace

When Dr. Robert H. Felix, the director of the National Institute of Mental Health, spoke at the dedication of the Health Center Chapel at the University of Florida, he said, "All of us are seeking peace of mind. By peace of mind, I do not necessarily mean freedom from worry or anxiety, but rather the acceptance of a way of thinking and living that draws us close to that peace of God which passes all understanding."[1]

As director of the National Institute of Mental Health, Dr. Felix is in a position to know. This is a realistic statement. It recognizes that one does not completely escape or evade worry and anxiety. This is certainly true in our restless generation. Also, he makes clear that the kind of peace that is needed is one based on faith. He quotes the Apostle Paul, who called it the "peace of God, which passes all understanding" (Phil. 4:7).

Ours is not the first generation for whom the need for peace has been a problem. A long time ago, Augustine experienced this same restlessness. No man ever phrased it more effectively. "Thou hast made us for Thyself, and our hearts are restless until they find their rest in Thee."

The Bible is filled with expressions of restlessness and frustration, but it also speaks of peace. Isaiah lived in a troubled and restless time, but he said:

[1]Robert H. Felix, M.D., "Religion and the Healthy Personality." *Pastoral Psychology,* Vol. XV, No. 148 (Nov., 1964), p. 10.

> Thou dost keep him in perfect peace,
> whose mind is stayed on thee, . . .
>
> —Isaiah 26:3

Paul lived in the midst of great tension. His letters were written to people who were subject to persecution, ostracism, and ridicule. The complete biblical passage that Dr. Felix referred to reads, "Have no anxiety about anything, but in everything by prayer and supplication with thanksgiving let your requests be made known to God. And the peace of God, which passes all understanding, will keep your hearts and your minds in Christ Jesus" (Phil. 4:6-7).

The desire for peace of mind is so universal in our day that it has produced a literature of its own called "peace of mind" literature. It has had a huge sale. This is understandable. If one can get peace of mind for $3.50 to $5.00, he is getting a good bargain.

The search for peace of mind has also had a rather large influence on preaching. Notice the sermon topics listed on the church page of a paper or in the journals of sermons. A sizable proportion of them are concerned with how to overcome worry, how to deal with anxiety, or how to attain inner peace. Some men seem to make this the major emphasis of their preaching. Much of this emphasis on peace of mind in literature and from the pulpit is cheap, shallow, and at times misleading.

Peace of mind sought for its own sake is an unworthy goal, one not true to the Christian gospel.

There are times when a person should be disturbed. Luther saw the corruption and evil within the church of his day, and he could have no peace. He had to take a stand.

Jacob A. Riis saw the slums of the "Mulberry Bend" district in New York, and he could have no peace until he wrote *How the Other Half Lives.*

129

Jesus went into the temple and saw money changers defrauding the people in the place of prayer, and he could have no peace until he had driven them out.

Peace of mind in the presence of injustice or evil is wrong, especially when possibilities for good exist. Such an attitude has caused some to be very critical of all attempts to find peace of mind—and not without reason.

There are times when peace of mind is self-defeating. To be contented with ourselves when we could do better is wrong. There are some people whose peace of mind should be disturbed. They never will attain their full potential until some of their self-satisfaction is removed.

Attaining peace of mind is not easy. This is one of the main criticisms of much of the literature, which seems to imply that the process is all quite simple. Men have attained an inner peace, but they did not do it quickly or easily.

Study the lives of the saints. Some of them had an inner serenity that is awe-inspiring, but it always came after years of seeking, after great personal discipline, sometimes after intense struggle. Any preaching on peace of mind should recognize this fact.

At the same time, to reject the whole idea is equally one-sided. Those people who are overly critical of "peace of mind" literature and "peace of mind" preaching are probably unconsciously wishing they had a bit of it.

Even those who are primarily interested in social reform should consider it. No one is going to be able to attack the evils of society for long unless he has some inner peace. Only he who operates from a secure base can carry on in the face of the discouragements and frustrations of any worthy social reform.

When Jesus said to the disciples, "Come away by yourselves to a lonely place, and rest awhile" (Mark 6:31), he was not telling them to escape but to regain strength. Isaiah was not evading the evils of his day when he said,

130

> Thou dost keep him in perfect peace,
> whose mind is stayed on thee, ...

One who desires to grow and attain his full strength does not do it all by striving. One grows by inner peace as much as by effort and by strain.

There is a positive, worthy, realistic approach to the fulfillment of this goal. Dr. Felix is right. All men seek peace, all men desire it, all men deserve it. Religion has much to say about it. It can and should be dealt with in preaching. Only the peace that comes through faith is a real and lasting peace. (1) Through preaching the pastor can make real the deep meaning of such biblical passages as,

> In returning and rest you shall be saved;
> in quietness and in trust shall be your strength.
>   —Isaiah 30:15

The message in this verse, and in similar verses, is needed in this restless time.

(2) Through preaching the pastor can counteract some of the fallacies and superficialities that characterize much popular literature. The man in the pulpit should point out the weaknesses of an inadequate philosophy, not perpetuate it. In so doing he can present a realistic understanding of inner serenity, one of man's most prized possessions.

(3) Through preaching the pastor can present illustrations and examples of men and women who have attained a profound inner serenity, often in the midst of most difficult circumstances. Paul, Augustine, Wesley, Woolman, Kagawa, and many others knew struggle, tension, and pressure, but they also knew serenity.

(4) Through preaching the pastor can present the spiritual conditions by which inner peace is found. As Dante expressed it, "In His will is our peace."

We have chosen the following two sermons precisely because their authors, Harry Emerson Fosdick and Harold Bosley, are men who spoke out courageously and honestly about the evils of their day. Neither could be accused of being sentimental or of desiring to escape the existing evils; yet both recognized the need for an inner sanctuary at the core of one's activity.

※

The High Uses of Serenity *

HARRY EMERSON FOSDICK

A FEW MILES from Wiscasset, in the State of Maine, is a beautiful, old New England meeting house which was dedicated to the worship of God about the time the Constitution of the United States was adopted. Separated now from any large center of population, it is generally closed, but once a year at least the countryside makes pilgrimage to worship in it. A few weeks ago, sitting in one of the old box pews, I listened to a well-known writer and student of English literature speaking on the influence of the New England meeting houses on the character of the Maine people. What most I recall, however, and expect never to forget, is a condensed statement evidently born out of long brooding over the classics of our English speech: "There is no great art without serenity." Even an amateur can

*From *The Power to See It Through* by Harry Emerson Fosdick. Copyright 1935 by Harper & Brothers. Reprinted by permission of Harper & Row, Publishers.

understand that. In music, literature, and painting, there is a difference between the fussiness and sensationalism of cheap and superficial work and the impression made on us by things supremely beautiful, and, when one stops to consider it, the speaker in that old New England meeting house was right. An essential element in all great art is serenity.

If some one says that great art has come out of troubled souls, as Chopin wrote his music often in an agony of creative turmoil, that is true, but the nocturnes themselves have poise, symmetry, proportion, peace, as truly as the Parthenon has, which even in its ruins fills the eye with rest.

If some one says that in their works, as well as in themselves, Wagner and Beethoven, Goethe and Shakespeare could be tumultuous and stormy, of course they could, but it was never like a tempest in a little pool roiling everything up, but always like a storm at sea, with wide distances around and undisturbed depths beneath. Think of the great music which we love the best, the great books which have meant most to us, the great paintings before which, if we could go back to Florence or Dresden, we would sit down quietly. The speaker was right. There is no great art without serenity.

Now, the highest of all arts is not music or literature or painting but life, and there, too, without serenity there can be nothing great.

This may be a dangerous thing to say, for nothing much more degenerating to character can be imagined than to make serenity an end in itself. One might almost as well make sleep an end in itself. No healthy person would do that. Sleep is not an end in itself, but it is a grand place to start from in the morning. A physical organism which has no background of tranquility can have no foreground of activity. That truth, translated from the physical to the spiritual plane, is, I should suppose, in days like these one of the most important that a man can get his eyes upon.

The high uses of serenity are plainly indicated in the family life. The members of a family ought to be engaged in many diversified and exciting enterprises; a home should be a beehive and in and out of it parents and children go on eager errands; all of which is gloriously possible if at the heart of the home there is serenity. Tennyson said about his wife: "The peace of God came into my life before the altar when I wedded her." When home means that, what great things may come out of it! When home lacks that, what great thing can come out of it? For here also the basic law holds good: nothing great without serenity.

Let us get our eye clearly, then, on what we are talking of—not serenity as an escape from life, but as an indispensable part of life, what rest is to the body, what peace is to the home, what roots are to the tree, what depth is to an ocean. Nothing in heaven above or the earth beneath great without it!

Consider, for one thing, that our personal happiness is profoundly involved in this. How much of happiness consists in interior serenity and how impossible is any happiness without it! Give us the loveliest of autumn days that the artistry of nature can create, with peaceful and resplendent trees around us and every circumstantial factor fortunate, yet even there a man cannot be happy if within him his spirit has lost its serenity. On the other hand, consider how strangely circumstanced some of our happy days have been, not set in autumnal trees or in

134

any fortunate environment, but in difficulty. Yet we were happy and the reason is plain—our spirits within us were serene.

If some one says that serenity is not the whole of happiness, that excitement, sensation, thrill are part of it, of course they are. Alas for a man who has nothing exciting to do or to enjoy, and who does not sometimes cast his harness off and have free pasturage to kick his heels in! Nevertheless, of all pathetic things few are worse than the familiar sight which one sees on every side in a town like this—people, I mean, who are trying to substitute thrills for serenity. Having no serenity at home within themselves, they run away into sensations, spend as much time as possible away from themselves amid their thrills, and then at last have to come back again to no serenity. That is the very essence of unhappiness.

On an average, twenty-two thousand people commit suicide in this country every year and the month when the largest number of them do it is May. It is a lovely month; all nature stirs with prophecies of coming summer—and they kill themselves. Moreover, for the most part it is not the poor and hard-put-to-it who do that. Listen to one of them who killed himself in the month of May: "I have had few real difficulties. I have had, on the contrary, an exceptionally glamorous life—as life goes—and I have had more than my share of affections and appreciations. . . . No one thing is responsible for this and no one person—except myself." Hearing that, what do we know about that man? Surely this much that, for all his excursions into life's successes and thrills, he kept coming back to a spirit where there was no serenity.

This human need for tranquility has always inhered in

life but in days like these it is accentuated. An Englishman is reported to have said that on three trips to the United States he came to three different conclusions as to what was the major passion of Americans. After one visit he concluded that this passion was power, after another he decided it was wealth, after the third he was sure it was acceleration. Well, acceleration is a towering fact among us. Speed becomes a mania and the pace is sometimes frantic, and in the midst of it one who cares about man's happiness and quality looks on the wreckage of that inner grace without which there can be nothing great in life or art, serenity.

In view of the prevalent unhappiness because of this, some of our modern sophisticates might well cease their attacks on our forefathers because they were dour, grim, and unhappy. Sometimes they doubtless were. Their theology at times was dreadful. But, while they may have been dour, grim, and unhappy, they were not cynical, flippant, futile, and unhappy. The more one deals with first-hand evidence, the more one is inclined to stake the Puritans themselves against many of our modern sophisticates in point of happiness.

A new biography of Louisa Alcott, author of *Little Women,* is just out—*Invincible Louisa.* One gets the impression that in her generation life was not so steady and calm or so dour and grim as we have pictured it. At any rate, in the first twenty-eight years of Louisa's life her family moved twenty-nine times, which is a record even for New York. Life then was not calm and easy. In the Alcott household it was very difficult. But one gets the impression also that it was happy, fundamentally happy; serenity in the soul, serenity in the home, something profound and peaceful in themselves and in their relationships with one another and with God—a haven to come back to from the storms of life. We moderns desperately need that and a vital Christianity gives it. For whatever else a real religion has done or left undone, it has ministered to those who understood it best a profound resource of inner power, a margin of reserve around their need, so that even in a prison Paul could sing about the "peace of God, which passeth all understanding." He had within himself a serene spirit to come home to. Without that, nothing in the world can give abiding happiness.

Consider also that not only personal happiness but personal character is involved in this. A great deal of our so-called modern badness is not malicious; it is simply life, lacking deep wells of quietness, trying to make up for the loss of serene meaning by plunging into sensations with a kick in them. When Dante turned his back, an exile, on his loved city of Florence, he described its wickedness as like the restlessness of a sick woman in a fever who keeps changing her posture to escape the pain. So, in a town like this, men plunge into debauchery and women fly from one sensation to another and live like whirling dervishes, for the same reason that small boys pull false fire alarms to feel the thrill of the converging fire engines. People behave so because they have missed something in their lives. The boys have missed the old and simpler happiness that some of us who lived in the countryside knew. They have no normal resources to fall back upon. And men and women who act like that have missed an inner quiet, a serene meaning in life that makes cheap sensation seem intolerably tawdry.

Some things we cannot imagine being cared for by a

man with any serenity of life. Why should he be attracted by drunkenness or by the hectic chances of a gambler's existence? Why should he find life's satisfaction in artificial excitements, with the hours between them but a dull interlude? This mad living, this constant change of posture to escape our pain, is a psychological compensation on the part of people who have missed serenity.

One of the finest things ever said by one man about another John Morley said about William Ewart Gladstone: "He was one of that high and favoured household who, in Emerson's noble phrase, 'live from a great depth of being.'" If that had been said about Gladstone by one of his coreligionists, it would not have been so impressive, but Morley was an agnostic; he was no coreligionist. Only, closely watching his lifelong friend, he saw where the secret of his moral power lay—he lived from a great depth of being. In a world like this and in a generation such as ours, there is no separating the problem of character from that. That pretty much *is* character.

Indeed, let a man ask himself what spoils serenity and he cannot answer without plunging deep into his moral life. Remorse ruins serenity; our infidelities, which we so eagerly anticipate and which pass from expectation through enjoyment into memory, haunt us evermore. Ill will spoils serenity, as does the cherished grudge, the mean vindictiveness. Jealousy wrecks serenity, as in the old story where, from the day he began enviously eyeing David, Saul never had a peaceful moment more. Engrossing ambition, where a man's ego becomes the clamorous center of the universe —that exiles serenity. Here we come to grips with our theme. Some at first may have supposed we were speaking of an easy virtue. No, one of the most costly. If serenity were easy there would be more of it. At its wicket gate there stand conditions to be satisfied—no unforgiven sins, no cherished grudges, no jealousy, no egoistic ambitions—the profound moral conditions of serenity.

To be sure, in this realm as in every other, there are caricatures and fakes. Man so instinctively knows that inward calm is to be desired that every conceivable device for getting it without fulfilling its serious conditions has been tried. One of the commonest, I suspect, is to seek a serene mind by shrugging one's shoulders at life, saying that nothing much matters anyway so that one need not bother much about anything. That provides a bogus serenity.

In Maine one summer, so Bishop Fiske writes, he and three friends spent a vacation with their guide, an old Maine fisherman. It was the summer when William Jennings Bryan was making his last attempt at the presidency and rock-ribbed Republican Maine was worried. One of the men in the party was a research physician; one was a geologist; another was an astronomer. They talked about the ages of the rocks and the evolution of life from the creatures of the sea and the immeasurable distances of the stars, and the Maine fisherman listened. At last even his taciturnity broke down and he poured out a flood of questions. Were the rocks really so old? Did life evolve from the sea creatures? Were the stars so far away? Was everything so inconceivably vast and ancient? And when at last he got it in his mind, he heaved a sigh of relief. "I guess," he said, "it won't make a powerful lot of difference even if William Jennings Bryan is elected!"

Such detachment born of a long look can have wholesomeness in it but it is not of that we are thinking now.

139

Rather, serenity is the basis of powerful activity. There is no art, no creativeness, no release of moral power even to rebuild society, without it. If a man is going to help lift the world he must have some solidity within him to lean his lever on. Some here doubtless said at first, In days of social and economic tension such as these, how can a man waste his time talking on serenity? I am thinking of these social questions. What else can an intelligent man think of in days like these? One who cares about them walks the streets and sees how few people are constructively and unselfishly thinking about public matters. How can they? They have no leisure from themselves. They have no serenity. They are harassed and agitated about themselves. They are afflicted with an appalling self-preoccupation. They have no inner steadiness to lean their levers on. And considering the case, one begins to understand some things not so clearly seen before.

Consider the Quakers, for example. Of all the Christian groups, which, would you say, has been right about more social questions than any other? The Quakers. Well, then, what have they stressed? It is very strange! They have stressed serenity—

> Dear Lord and Father of mankind,
> Forgive our feverish ways.

Yet when we stop to think of it, is it so strange? Can we think of any supreme soul in history without this quality within him? We cannot understand Christ without it. When he talks about inward peace one well may listen. A young man he was, dangerously plunging into revolutionary matters that would shake the world; yet he talked about inward peace. He never could have done anything without it. In the Garden of Gethsemane he might have lost it. That was the struggle under the olive trees, to maintain his serenity. Everything depended on it. There was a victory when he was sure of it, the interior leverage of the divine Archimedes by which he moved the world. It is of that we are talking. Lacking it, there is no powerful character, and it belongs only to those who live from a great depth of being.

So, inevitably, we come to our third fact: not only are personal happiness and personal character involved in this but personal religion. Some time since, an invitation came to attend a conference of humanists, non-theistic humanists, who are trying to build churches on a moral program only, and I was asked to tell them frankly what I thought was the trouble with the humanists. It was impossible to go but, could I have done so, I know what I would have said in candid criticism of my humanistic friends. All profound religion ministers to three basic human needs: the need of a great metaphysic, a philosophy of life to put meaning into living; the need of a great morality, principles of conduct, personal and social, to ennoble living; the need of a great mysticism, profound resources of interior power by which to live. All profound religion has made to life these three major contributions: a great philosophy, a great ethic, a great resource of power. The trouble with the humanists is that they are trying to limp along with one of them, the ethic. All complete religion has three dimensions. It has height, an elevated philosophy of life; it has depth, a profound resource for life; it has extension, a noble way of living life. The trouble with the humanists is that they try to keep it one-dimensional, to preserve the moral extension without the height of faith or the depth of power, and I, for one, am certain that that essentially is incomplete and that, for psychological reasons, if for nothing else, it will not work.

Humanism, however, is more than an organized movement. It is a modern mood, an attitude, a drift that affects us all, so that every Sunday these pews have people in them powerfully tempted to a one-dimensional Christianity of moral demand only. Then, when trouble comes, people have no high philosophy of life or deep resources of power to give serenity. And sometimes, alas, they discover that, in facing heavy hours, bearing heavy griefs, handling heavy tasks, when a man loses serenity he loses everything.

I plead today for a kind of religion which helps a man to live from a great depth of being. You young people in particular, eager, enthusiastic, devoted, as many of you are, to the noblest causes of today, beware of a Christianity that merely adds one more demand on life without being a resource for life. The demands of life are terrific enough already. As the years pass they often mount appallingly. What if, then, a man has a Christianity which merely piles on him a further demand for more sacrifice and more toil but which does not at the same time help him to meet the demand from a great depth of being? There is much eager, youthful, one-dimensional Christianity like that today.

My friends, if we are to have a profound religion we may indeed throw away our old, childish, anthropomorphic ideas of God, but we may not throw away God and leave ourselves caught like rats in the trap of an aimless, meaningless, purposeless universe. There is nothing in that

142

philosophy of life to help a man live from a profound depth of being. And while we may throw away our early, ignorant ideas of prayer, we may not throw away prayer, the flowing of internal fountains that keep their freshness when all the superficial cisterns peter out. These are the other dimensions of religion which, helping us to meet demand with resource amid the strain of life, bestow serenity.

Young man or woman, some day you are going to be forty years old, fifty years old, sixty years old, and the years between now and then will not be easy, either. We will take it for granted that morally you will try to live a good life and socially a useful one. All *that* I pray for you, and something more beside, that as age comes on you may deserve the salutation which in the old days of titled nobility stood high on the list—'Your Serene Highness.' After a long life, that is a crown of praise—Your Serene Highness.

❧

When I Am With God *

HAROLD A. BOSLEY

Scripture Lesson: Psalm 19

I

WHEN A DISTINGUISHED psychiatrist referred to us as a "neurotic age," the facts were all on his side. The rapid and, as yet, unchecked increase in ailments due to emo-

*From *Sermons on the Psalms* by Harold Bosley. Copyright 1955 by Harper & Brothers. Reprinted by permission of Harper & Row, Publishers.

tional disturbance and tension is one of the acknowledged scandals of modern civilization as well as one of the greatest perplexities of medical science. The boast frequently heard half a century ago that the increase in leisure-time activities and vacation periods would make us a happier, healthier people has been silenced by grim facts. We may live longer than we used to, but it is yet to be proved that our longer lives are happier, more useful, more satisfying, more creative than the shorter ones of our fathers. We are a nervous, taut, hard-pressed, harried, easily upset, easily irritated and easily exhausted generation. We have not learned how to avoid unwholesome tensions; we have not learned how to manage or reduce them once we get them— or they get us. And they distort our view, our energies, and usually paralyze thought and action with fear at precisely the times when they are needed most.

Facts like these prompted the physician, Alexis Carrell, to observe that man simply does not have the nervous equipment to keep pace with modern civilization.

Not all physicians give us up as hopeless, though. A number of years ago a prominent doctor advised us to regard the management of tensions as one of the major health problems of our time. He said that there were three things to do about it.

First, "look *inside* yourself"—understand the glandular meaning of fear, anger, worry and hate; realize that these emotions actually upset the balance of the entire system in so radical a fashion that they can and will lead to nervous breakdown if indulged in too frequently. Second, "look *at* yourself," says the doctor. He documents this in a remorseless way: "If we who rush and worry needlessly could see ourselves as others see us, simple pride would stop us. Let

144

any morbidly distraught woman consult her mirror when she is under the lash of our . . . [emotional] tyrants, her face ugly with frowns, her jaws clenched. Cosmetic tricks won't banish those beauty destroyers." Third, "look *away* from yourself. Practice lifting your mind, every now and again, above the rush and confusion around you. Take time out during your busiest day to think of something pleasant."[1]

I am quite willing to let the physicians look inside us and the beauty experts look at us, but there is something religious faith wants to say about the third—looking away from ourselves. This suggests one answer to the question of the place of devotion in life. The value of this look away from ourselves will depend entirely upon what we look at. The doctor suggests we look at something pleasant. So far, so good, I suppose, but surely we can do better than that! At least historic religion thinks so. It advises us to look away from ourselves by looking toward God.

"I will lift up mine eyes unto the hills. Whence cometh my help? My help cometh from the Lord who made heaven and earth"—is one way of putting it. Another is the 19th Psalm—read earlier in the service—which bids us look away from ourselves not that we may simply enjoy something or other but that we may contemplate and stand in awe of the glory of God, the Creator of all, and rejoice in His care for and mercy toward us. Never has the religious look away from oneself been put in more personal and sensitive terms than these: "Let the words of my mouth and the meditation of my heart be acceptable in thy sight, O Lord, my rock and my redeemer."

Here is the very heart of religious devotion: An aware-

---

[1]Richard H. Hoffmann, M.D., "Tension's Little Trigger Men." *The American Weekly* (July 15, 1951). Used by permission of W. R. Hearst, Jr.

ness of God, an awareness of one's dependence upon Him, a sincere acceptance of that relationship. Here is a man—a person like any one of us—honestly and humbly looking away from himself, looking toward God, then in the strength of that, coming back for another look at himself.

II

Once we see what devotion is, what it means, we will make a place for it in our daily life—of that I have no doubt.

Devotion, in a word, is the conscious, habitual effort to look toward God. It is that period in our day when we try to center our thoughts on God, when, through meditation and prayer, we approach Him in a deeply personal way.

The nun reading her prayers as she hurtles toward the loop on the El is engaged in devotion. The man who at a stated time each day reads his Bible and repeats a prayer is engaged in devotions. The person who comes into a chapel for meditation and prayer is engaged in devotions. I have never found a better interpretation of what devotion means to one who practices it than Walter Rauschenbusch's poem, "The Postern Gate":

In the castle of my soul
Is a little postern gate,
Whereat, when I enter,
I am in the presence of God.
In a moment, in the turning of a thought,
I am where God is.
This is a fact.[2]

[2]From *A Biography of Walter Rauschenbusch* by Dores Robinson Sharpe, The Macmillan Company, Publisher. Used by permission.

And then the poet suggests several meanings of this great fact:

This world of ours has length and breadth,
A superficial and horizontal world.
When I am with God
I look deep down and high up,
And all is changed.

How changed? For one thing, we sense anew the mystery of life, the vastness of the universe, the glory of our privilege of sharing in it. Most of us get so busy with programs and plans and schedules and techniques that we forget the ancient affirmation, "Be still, and know that I am God!" We are so preoccupied with our problems, worries, fears and hates that we forget to "worship the Lord in the beauty of holiness"— or in any other way at all, for that matter. We forget to worship, period. And when we do, life gets wholly out of perspective.

The late H. G. Wells was one of the most gifted men of his generation: brilliant mind, tireless student, keen prophet and an excellent writer. But there was a puzzling despair and doubt hovering over all that he wrote. The longer he lived the gloomier he became until, in his last public interview, he gave up the cause of civilization as hopeless. Wells gives us the clue to his morbid outlook in this autobiographical note, "There was a time when my little soul shone and was uplifted at the starry enigma of the sky. That has gone absolutely. Now I can go out and look at the

147

stars as I look at the pattern of wallpaper on a railway station waiting room."

What a falling off that is from the Psalmist's awed cry, "The heavens are telling the glory of God; and the firmament proclaims his handiwork." John Ruskin was right when he hurled this challenge at a generation that thought the meaning of life could be found in the accumulation of wealth, "I would sooner live in a cottage and wonder at everything, than live in Warwick Castle and wonder at nothing."

How long will it take us to learn that when we begin to lose our sense of the mystery of life we shall soon be losing our grip on the meaning of life? And when that happens a good deal of adolescent and half-hysterical bragging is certain to take place about the glory of man. We begin to chant with Swinburne,

Glory to man in the highest
For man is the master of things.

And we wind up dropping atomic bombs all over the world.

One can be proud of the progress man has made, can rejoice in his many rich achievements, and still know that the glory of man is a poor substitute for the glory of God. And no one has known this more truly or stated it more fearlessly than the men whom we gladly acknowledge to be our greatest. They, at least, have no intention of posing as God! "Why callest thou me good?" the greatest of all demanded; "There is none good but one, even God!"

Lose that sense of the mystery of life surrounding us personally and overarching the generations, and we will have lost more than a desire to worship God; we will soon lose our reason for hope and faith in man, including ourselves.

> When I am with God
> I look deep down and high up,
> And all is changed.

III

The poet suggests another value of devotion—one we have been anticipating in what we have just been saying,

> When I enter into God,
> All life has a meaning.

It is God's meaning for life that we always seek and sometimes find in our devotions. There is no way of estimating the difference this discovery makes in a number of very concrete ways. It gives us a new answer to the question, "Who am I?"

One of the most poignant lines in *The Death of a Salesman* is Willie Loman's insistence, "I have a right to know who I am." Of course he does. So does every man. One of the marks of maturity is the exercise of this right in a thoroughly responsible fashion. But how did Willie Loman try to discover who he was? By looking inside himself, at himself, and never away from himself and never, never, toward God. He was looking for the right thing in the wrong place and in the wrong way. Is it any wonder that he found nothing worth living for, that despair and defeat are the final movements in his spiritual—or should we say "spiritless"—pilgrimage?

Religion has a conviction, one born of and bolstered by thousands of years of human experience, that life has real meaning, God's meaning; that the Willie Lomans of this world, asking after it, can find it at least in part; and that in the finding of it we can discover who we are.

As we look away from ourselves, looking toward God in a spirit of devotion, we discover several important facts about life. We discover God as the Creator of all, the One in whom "we live and move and have our being," "Our Father." This is the true setting of life, and we must see ourselves in it if we would discover the real meaning of our life. The glory of religious faith is the way it sets everyone and everything against this backdrop of eternity. Sincere devotion guides us to the knowledge that we are the children of God; it never permits us to think that we are god. We begin then with the simple assurance that the most important thing about us, and it ought to be the most important thing to us, is God's purpose in creating us. Once see ourselves as the children of God, and we cannot escape the conviction that we ought so to regard all other men and ought to judge our relationships with them by that fact.

> When I enter into God,
> All life has a meaning—

A meaning in which

> Big things become small, and small things become great.
> The near becomes far, and the future is near.
> The lowly and despised is shot through with glory.

What fairer fruit of devotion could one seek than this: A vision of the true worth of what we do day by day? Every preacher needs it, I know. And I am sure every businessman, every parent, and every student needs it too. It is appallingly easy to get all mixed up about the relative worth of what we do. When that happens, chaos moves in. We find ourselves measuring the worth of our lives by the number of organizations we belong to rather than by the quality of what we contribute to them and through them. Mothers bemoan the time their families take, thinking they would rather spend it at the bridge table or on the golf links, or even in church organizations. Husbands and wives count a quiet evening at home as "lost" and wish for a continuous whirl of activities outside the house. Students feel that they are missing out on a lot if they concentrate on their studies and give little time to the blinding whirl of campus life.

If we are not aware of this danger and on guard against it, we will become "hollow men," empty of purpose, and empty of any sense of real value at all.

I cannot say that the habit of daily devotion is a guarantee that this will not happen, but I can say that it is the best guarantee we have. It reminds me of a small boy's description of what salt is: "Salt is what spoils the potatoes when you leave it out." Devotion is what spoils life when we leave it out. When we put it in and put it in regularly we have our best chance to keep our values in order, our lives in proportion, and our vision of life's meaning bright and beautiful.

The poet assures us, further, that devotion is as deeply social as it is intensely personal:

When I am in the consciousness of God,
My fellowmen are not far-off and forgotten,
But close and strangely dear.

. . . .

They shine, as if a light were glowing within them.
Even those who frown on me
And love me not
Seem part of the great scheme of Good.

Devotion, then, is more than the effort of man to re-
discover God and himself; it results, consciously or not, in
the rediscovery of the true brotherhood of all men.

Most of us believe in the brotherhood of man but in a
limited sort of way. That is, we want to pick the brothers
who are to be admitted. And when the picking is over we
have admitted those who think as we do, believe as we do,
perhaps even pray and look as we do.

The brotherhood of man that great religion talks about
is a quite different thing. It actually includes all men, no
matter who they are or what they have done. The brotherhood of man that we discover in devotion is of this sort. It
includes all—even our enemies. Until one has made that
discovery for himself through religious experience it is hard
to get him to see that it is not only possible but inescapable.
Yet it is possible to feel a deep sense of oneness with, understanding of and sympathy with, those who on the surface
appear to be our enemies. Most of us hesitate over it
though, feeling a little like the son who was exasperated by
his wonderful mother's determination to see good in even
bad people. "Mother," he exclaimed, "I think you could
see good in the devil himself." To which she replied in-
stantly and gravely, "Well, he is persistent."

If we are fond of our fears, our hates and our prejudices,
let us stay away from the practice of looking toward God,
for in the long run, it will undermine them all by digging
down to the firm foundation of the brotherhood of all

men—and once there, it will demand that we build a life and a society worthy of the foundation.

Let those who have engaged in it speak about the cleansing and strengthening of mind and spirit that come through the practice of devotion.

> My fever is gone
> In the great quiet of God.
> My troubles are but pebbles on the road,
> My joys are like the everlasting hills.

Judge Harold R. Medina who presided at the trial of the eleven Communist leaders in New York in 1949 made an address before a group of churchmen some months later. He told how the tension and torment of that sensational case had worn him to the breaking point. Finally, he said,

. . . I finally had to leave the courtroom and lie down in my chambers. Let me be frank: I was thinking then that perhaps I should never go back. In my weakness it seemed to me at last that I had stood as much as I could for as long as I could. I could not endure more of it. I was ready to give up.

But, instead, like a frightened child calling to his father in the dark, I asked God to take charge of things and that His will be done. I cannot report any mysterious or supernatural experience as a result of that prayer. All I know is that, as I lay on the couch in the heat of that darkened chamber, some kind of new strength seemed to flow into my veins. That brief period of communion with my Maker saved my life and saved the trial. After 15 minutes I was refreshed, and went back to carry on the business of my court.

And I gained in strength from that moment on to the end. For Someone else was with me, all the way.[3]

---

[3]Judge Harold R. Medina, "Someone Else on the Bench." *Reader's Digest* (August, 1951), p. 18. Used by permission.

Looking toward God can give us at least a portion of peace with the work of each day that seems to have been felt by John Wesley and St. Francis of Assisi. Both were asked essentially the same question and made essentially the same answer.

When John Wesley was asked by a lady how he would spend his time if he knew he would die at twelve o'clock the next day at midnight, he answered, "Why, just as I had expected to spend the time. I would preach at Gloucester tonight and tomorrow morning, at Tewkesbury in the afternoon, go to my friend Martin's house for entertainment, converse and pray with the family as usual, retire to my room at ten o'clock, commend myself to my heavenly Father, lie down to rest, and wake up in glory."

St. Francis was hoeing in his garden when the question was put to him by an ardent follower as to what he would do if he were suddenly to learn that he were to die at sunset that very day. He replied, "I would finish hoeing my garden."

When I am with God, life takes on new meaning—this is the unqualified testimony of those who in the fine old phrase have "practiced the presence of God" daily. I can think of many great gifts parents might give their children, but I can think of no greater gift than this: That by their habit, by their example and by their admonition their children shall learn the meaning, the worth, the strength of devotion; that something of the power, the direction and the poise that can come only through this practice of the presence of God will be a part of their daily life.

Yet there is a sense in which it is misleading to say, "When I am with God." Strictly, we are with Him all of the time. We cannot get away from Him. This is His universe, His world, His life that we live—not ours. He surrounds us as the sunlight surrounds the houses in which we live. Yet we live in darkness. We have let care, worry, fear and hatred pull down the blinds of our minds and seal the doors of our lives until we seem to be lost, alone, forsaken. But it is a lostness, an aloneness, a forsakenness of our own making, not of God's. For He wants to enter in and have communion with us—but we must open the door.

> Grant us such grace that we may work thy will
> And speak thy word and walk before thy face.
> Profound and calm, like waters deep and still;
> Grant us such grace.[4]

---

[4]Christina Georgina Rossetti.

From Pride to Humility

🌸 🌸 🌸

If a pastor would ask his people to submit a list of their greatest needs, probably few would include humility. It is a need nonetheless; at least the biblical writers saw it as such. In the Book of Isaiah it says:

> For thus says the high and lofty One
>   who inhabits eternity, whose name is Holy:
> "I dwell in the high and holy place,
>   and also with him who is of a contrite and humble spirit,
>   . . ."
>
> —Isaiah 57:15

The prophet Micah, speaking of the requirements of God, said:

> . . . what does the Lord require of you,
>   but to do justice, and to love kindness,
> and to walk humbly with your God?
>
> —Micah 6:8

Such passages put the value of humility in a very significant category. It is seen here not as a simple virtue but as a quality which God himself approves.

Jesus spoke often of humility. He saw it as a mark of true greatness. One day when the apostles were arguing over which of them was the greatest, Jesus placed a child in their midst and said, "Whoever humbles himself like this child, he is the greatest in the kingdom of heaven" (Matthew 18:4).

On another occasion, when Jesus noticed how people clamored for places of recognition and distinction, he told a story which concluded with this sentence, "For every one who exalts himself will be humbled, and he who humbles himself will be exalted" (Luke 14:11), the same words with which he concluded the parable of the Pharisee and the publican.

Throughout the Bible there is a constant emphasis on the dangers of pride and the value of humility, for "God opposes the proud, but gives grace to the humble" (Jas. 4:6; 1 Pet. 5:5).

Much pride is a defense. A man who boasts and brags may really be saying, "I feel insecure." To condemn him for his lack of humility does no good. What he needs is help in overcoming his feelings of inadequacy so that he no longer needs to use such defenses.

Genuine humility does not mean a lack of confidence. One of the problems in preaching on humility arises because so many people think of humility as being a negative virtue, displayed by a "timid soul" who has no convictions, no strength.

Actually, humility is an indication of strength. The great artist, the great surgeon, or the great scholar knows he has knowledge, skill, and ability such as few men have; he is confident of what he can do, but he is humble about it.

When humility is lacking, one cuts himself off from life's greatest rewards—friendship, growth, the love of God. Nothing separates a man from his fellowmen more quickly than conceit, pride, haughtiness, disdain. Henry Churchill King said, "A teachable humility is the first condition of all possible growth." In the Bible pride is seen as a sin. It separates man

157

from God, but its opposite, a humble spirit, is a basic demand of both the Old and New Testaments.

(1) Through preaching one can make clear the values of humility and the warnings against pride as expressed in the Bible.

(2) Through preaching one can save humility from the caricatures in which it is often thought and presented.

(3) Through preaching one can help people attain humility often when he is not preaching on humility at all. Humility, like happiness, does not come as a result of direct attack. It comes as a by-product of many other things. It grows out of penitence and an awareness of one's own weaknesses and limitations. It grows out of a realization of man's indebtedness to others. It comes as a result of an attempt to be of service when one realizes the finitude of his own wisdom, the magnitude of the task, and the limits of his efforts. Humility comes as a result of the recognition of a power greater than oneself to whom we are all indebted.

Humility comes out of genuine worship when one becomes conscious of the majesty and love of God. After one catches a glimpse of the sacrifice, the spirit of Christ, he "pours contempt on all his pride."

Whenever a pastor makes any of these experiences real, he helps his people move from pride to humility.

Humility is not a subject on which many sermons are preached. Perhaps this is because preachers, too, do not sense its need or perhaps because it is not a very exciting subject. But it is an important one. At least Phillips Brooks thought so and preached a sermon called "Humility." Donald Baillie preached on the subject of pride; in fact, he related it to the grace of God.

158

❧

Humility *

PHILLIPS BROOKS

"And be clothed with humility."—1 Peter 5:5

WE ARE THINKING, during Lent, about the duty of being humble. But what a poor thing we make out of humility. What a fiction it is apt to be with us. How artificial we are apt to make it. We reduce it to a few observances. We try to cultivate it from outside. At most we try to school ourselves into certain feelings, making ourselves think about certain things until we reach a certain emotional condition, and we call that humility; but humility not as an action, not as a sentiment, but as an abiding character, out of which all actions should flow in one direction, from which all sentiments should rise, cloud-like, with one color,—this we hardly conceive of, and to seek after it hardly enters into our thoughts.

Let us look, then, at humility a little while, and see if we cannot get some deeper and truer notions about what it really is, and where it really comes from. It is not well to use the word, and praise the grace, and yet be all the while mistaking what it is that we name and praise.

The word itself and its history are interesting. "There are cases," says Coleridge, "in which more knowledge, of more value, may be conveyed by the history of a word than

*From *Sermons* by Phillips Brooks, copyright 1876, E. P. Dutton & Company.

by the history of a campaign." You can often trace a word down the generations and judge of the character of each period by seeing whether the word was popular or unpopular, whether it was a title of dishonor or of honor in each successive age; just as, if you could send a great warrior or a great thinker or a great saint, a Caesar or a Bacon or a St. John, from age to age and country to country, and could see how every age and country regarded Him, you would have a test of the character of every land and time. It is true of the careers of the best words, as Jesus said it was to be of the progress of His disciples, that "he that receiveth you receiveth me." The best and noblest words are really the judges of the people, who pronounce on their own moral condition as they speak them with affection or dislike.

Now take this word humility. It was not a new word when the New Testament was written. It, or its Greek equivalent, was very common. It had been used for years. Only it is striking that almost without exception the word humility, used before the time of Christ, is used contemptuously and rebukingly. It always meant meanness of spirit. To be humble was to be a coward. It described a cringing soul. It was a word of slaves. Such is its almost constant classic use.

Where could we find a more striking instance of the change that the Christian religion brought into the world, than in the way in which it took this disgraceful word and made it honorable. To be humble is to have a low estimation of one's self. That was considered shameful in the olden time. Nobody claimed it for himself. Nobody enjoined it upon another. You insulted a man if you called him humble. It seemed to be inconsistent with that self-respect which is necessary to any good activity. Christ came and made the despised quality the crowning grace of the culture that He inaugurated. Lo! the disgraceful word became the key-word of His fullest gospel. He redeemed the quality, and straightway the name became honorable. It became the ambition of all men to wear it. To call a man humble was to praise him now. Men affected it if they did not have it. Pride began to ape humility when humility was made the crowning grace of human life.

It is in moral changes such as these, in alterations of the standards and aspirations of the race, that the revolutionary power of Christianity is really shown, far more than in external changes, the progress of civilization, the reshaping of empires. Think what the change must have been. Think with what indignation and contempt men of the old school in Rome and Athens must have seen mean-spiritedness, as they called it, taken up, inculcated and honored, proclaimed as the salvation of the world, and Him in whom it was most signally embodied made the Saviour and King of men. Ah, it seems to me more and more that it must have been very hard for those early disciples to have believed in Christ.

But let us see, if we can, what the change was that Christianity accomplished, and how it came about. The quality that Christianity rescued and glorified was humility. Humility means a low estimate or value of one's self. But all values are relative. The estimate we set on anything depends of course on the standard with which we compare it. You cannot tell how big anything is, unless you compare it with something else, and so values are always varying as the standards or the objects with which you compare the thing that you are valuing change. Your boy of twelve plays with his little brothers of three or four, and seems to them a giant and a sage, then he goes and sits among his teachers, and is forthwith a child again. Everything depends for its value on the standards with which you compare it. The silver is precious till you find the gold, the gold until you find the diamond.

Now Christianity's great primary revelation was God. Much about Him it showed men; but first of all it showed them Him. He, the Creator, the Governor, became a presence clear and plain before men's hearts. His greatness, His holiness, His love,—nay, we cannot describe Him by His qualities, for He is greater than them all,—He, by the marvellous method of the Incarnation, showed himself to man. He stood beside man's work. He towered above and folded Himself about man's life. He entered into men's closets and took possession of men's hearts. And what then? God in the world must be the standard of the world. Greatness meant something different when men had seen how great He was, and the manhood which had compared itself with lesser men and grown proud now had a chance to match itself with God, and to see how small it was and to grow humble about itself.

We are not dealing only with history; we are not talking only about what happened eighteen hundred years ago. A man is living a pagan life here, now, among us. Wherever he goes he meets men whom he measures himself against, and finds that he surpasses them. He is the strongest man in the wrestle of business, the quickest man at a bargain, the wittiest man at an argument. Now that man cannot be humble. He overtops his little world and he must think high. The White Mountains have never seen the Alps, and Mount Washington and Mount Jefferson, looking down and our skill, just suppose that suddenly Omniscience towered up above our knowledge, and Omnipotence above our strength, and the Infinite Wisdom stood piercing out of the sight of our ignorant and baffled skill. Must it not crush the man with an utter insignificance? What is the use of heaving up these mole-hills so laboriously close by the gigantic mountain-side? But if the revelation is not only this; if it includes not only the greatness but the love of God; if the majesty that is shown to us is the majesty of a father, which takes our littleness into its greatness, makes it part of itself, honors it, trains it, does not mock it, then there comes the true graciousness of humility. It is not less humble, but it is not crushed. It is not paralyzed, but stimulated. The energy which the man used to get out of his estimate of his own greatness he gets now out of the sight of His Father's, which yet is so near to him that, in some finer and higher sense, it still is his; and so he is more hopeful and happy and eager in his humility than he ever used to be in his pride. This is the philosophy of reverence and humility as enrichers of life and main-springs of activity.

There is nothing so bad for man or woman as to live always with their inferiors. It is a truth so important that one might well wish to turn aside a moment and urge it, even in its lower aspects, upon the young people who are just making their associations and friendships. Many a temptation of laziness or pride induces us to draw towards those who do not know as much or are not in some way as strong as we are. It is a smaller tax upon our powers to be in their society. But it is bad for us. I am sure that I have known men, intellectually and morally very strong, the whole development of whose intellectual and moral life has suffered and been dwarfed, because they have only

He asserted and magnified the essential glory of humanity. Remember, always, when you say that Christ convicted man of sin, that, nevertheless, true as that is, there never was any life that so superbly asserted the essential worth of humanity,—showed what a surpassing thing it is to be a man,—like that sin-convicting life of Jesus. He showed us that the human might be joined with the divine. He showed us that from lips of flesh like ours those mighty words, "I and my Father are one," might issue, and yet the lips not be burned up in uttering them; and more than this, He showed us that the human soul was worth all the mysterious and terrible redemption of the cross. Thus He glorified human nature. And does it seem strange then to say that by this glorification He taught man that it was his true place to be humble? Ah, if a man must be humbled, and is exalted by his humility, when he sees God, surely when he sees the possibility of himself, there is no truer or more exalted feeling for him than to look in on what he is and think it very mean and wretched by the side of what he might be, what his Lord has showed him that he was made for. Christ makes us humble by showing us our design. Again, let me suppose that I can really get close to the proud, self-sufficient master of the state, the shop, the farm. I get his ear in some lull of his noisy work, and I tell him the story of a being whom God loves and treasures. I tell him about powers meant to grapple with eternal things. I describe to him a love that is made to love the loveliest. I open the gates of immortality and show him life opening, brightening forever and forever. I am able to touch the very breast of the Almighty, and lo! the crystal window of revelation opens and the love of God for this wonderful being burns clear within. "God so loved the world!" I tell the world has known no psalms and no lamentations like the Bible's, and they are parts of the one same book.

If I am speaking directly to the experience of any thoughtful and sensitive person here today, I know that he will bear me witness when I say that in this great characteristic of it Christianity is true to all the deepest facts of human life. Have you not learnt, did you not learn very early, that exaltation and abasement do not stand far part in, do not come singly into, your life? Thoughtless and coarse natures, feeling only the grosser delights and the grosser sorrows, are either all delighted or all sorrowful, and know no mixture of emotions. Either they are all triumphant or entirely discouraged. But as you went farther and came to subtler disciplines of God, have you not known what it was to see your privileges never so clearly as in the light of your imperfections, and your imperfections never so clearly as in the light of your privileges? Just when you saw some dear life pass through the gate into the immortal world, and saw what a bliss and triumph there must be for one to whom that unseen world was real and bright, just then you felt how little you had grasped it, how wedded you were to these things that are mortal and seen. Just when you saw some glimpse of the sweetness and beauty of giving up yourself for others, you found how unwilling you were to sacrifice yourself, how full of selfishness you were. The same light which showed you the heaven that you were made for has always showed you the rock that you were chained to; as the same word of Jesus which showed the young nobleman the treasures in heaven brought back before his mind the treasures on earth from which he could not tear himself away. This makes the sacredness and awfulness of life when we come to know it,

168

that we are never so near our highest as when we are most sensible of the danger of our lowest, and the danger of the lowest is never so real to us as when the splendor of the highest stands wide open.

I think we cannot but see the beauty of a humility like this if it once becomes the ruling power of a changed man's life, this humility born of the sight of a man's possible self. It has in it all that is good in the best self-respect. Nay, with reference to the whole subject of self-respect this seems to be true, that the only salvation from an admiration of our own present condition, which is pride, is to be found in a profound respect for the best possibility and plan of our being, which involves humility. Ask yourself. You are dealing, say, with one of the proud, successful men of whom our land is full, a man successful in some one of the low and sordid planes of effort in which men are forever struggling. He is proud of his smartness, proud of his sharp, hard unscrupulousness. Suppose you had, for instance, the mere successful politician of the day. The man admires himself. To him there is nothing in all the world conceivable so fine and complete as the sort of life that he is living. That is his vulgar pride. Will you make that man humble? You may hold up before him the most shining characters the world has ever seen. Marshal the white, unstained names before him and they do not abash him. He easily counts them his inferiors. You never can abash him till in some way he becomes conscious of a purer, honester, and nobler self. Never until by some shock or other his life is broken and he sees what he might have been, sees what he might be. In some stillness of the night when a better nature is called out by God, and a man whom he recognizes as himself and yet who shames the self that lived his yesterday, stands visible before him, then he is humbled. In some revival meeting when a picture of heaven or a picture of hell, painted with graphic earnestness, reaches him and lets him see this soul of his which he has kept truckling for dollars or for offices is capable of heaven and capable of hell, when the dignity of his responsibility is set before him, then he is humbled.

Let us be sure that there is, laid up in the heart of God, an image and a thought of each of us, which if we could see it would shame and humble us. We go on our way, we sin and rejoice in sinning, we love low things, we starve our souls or we pollute them, we wade through mire and grovel in idleness; but all the while there lies God's thought of us, before which if we saw it we must be ashamed. The Christian pilgrims to the Jordan are baptized there sometimes in a pure white robe, which then is laid by to be used again for the purpose of their burial. They are to be wrapped in it again when they are dead. After all the sins and miseries and vicissitudes of earth are over, they must come back at last and meet that symbol of the purity with which they started their new life. And often, with that robe laid up at home, they must stop in the midst of some foul passage of their life, and remember how white it is, and be humiliated. So it is the sight of what God meant us to be that makes us ashamed of what we are. And it is the death of Christ for us, the preciousness that He saw in our souls making them worthy of that awful sacrifice, it is that which lets us see our own soul as He sees it in its possibility, and so lets us see it in its reality as he sees it too and put our pride away and be humble.

I have spoken of the way in which Christianity sets a man humbly before God and humbly before himself. The name too, Christ has died. This is the sublime revelation of his faith about his fellows. And when he sees them thus, he sees the true use of these powers, of all this life that God has given him. To serve this hidden life of all his brethren, to help it out into some sort of consciousness and action, this is the object to which he wants to dedicate his saved soul, to the salvation of the souls of others. And this is his humility. Honor your own life as much as you will, only see in the lives of other men a value and essential dignity that makes them worthy of your giving yourself up to their help and culture, and then you are the humble man. If you believe with all your heart that there is nothing in you too good to be employed in the divine work of helping some lost child of God back to the Father, then you have really learnt the humility of Christ. Do you remember Him? The supper was ended, and strangely on that solemn night the disciples had fallen into an untimely quarrel about which of them should be the greatest, and then the Lord Himself rose from the table and tied the towel round His waist, and went from one wondering disciple to another and washed the feet of all. And then He interpreted His own parable: "If I, your Lord and Master, have washed your feet, ye ought also to wash one another's feet." Did Jesus compare Himself with each of those disciples, and own Himself the inferior of each? He only said by His exquisite action that there was something in every one of them, in serving which even His divinity found no inappropriate employment. It was the truth of His whole Incarnation wrought into a homely picture. And the humility of Christ's disciples, as He said, is one in nature with His own. The delicate woman for very love of Christ nursing Christ's lowest brethren in the most dreadful wards of the hospital; the brave missionary living his squalid life among the Indians in their wigwams; the mother giving her life for the child the Lord has given her; what is the power in them all but this, the certainty that every one of Christ's brethren is worthy of the consecration of the very best that Christ's disciple has to give? Does that seem hard for you to believe? Have you grown weary of looking for any signs of promise in this dull mass of fellow-men and withdrawn yourself into some luxury of self-culture, feeling as if what you had and were was too good to be wasted upon such creatures as these sick and poor and ignorant? You must be rescued from this proud conceit, not simply by counting yourself lower, but by valuing more highly the spiritual natures of these fellow-men. You must value them as He valued them, who gave His life for them, before you can be as humble in their presence as He was; and that can come only by making yourself their servant. Only he who puts on the garment of humility finds how worthily it clothes his life. Only he who dedicates himself to the spiritual service of his brethren, simply because his Master tells him they are worth it, comes to know how rich those natures of his brethren are, how richly they are worth the total giving of himself to them.

This seems to me to be the ever-increasing joy of the minister's life, if one may venture for once to speak of his own work. A man becomes a minister because God says, "Go speak in the temple the words of this life." He begins the service of his fellow-men in pure obedience to God's command, but the joy and ever-richening delight of the minister's work is in finding how deep this human soul to which his Lord has sent him really is. The nature to which he ministers, as he meets its exhibitions here and there, is always amazing him with its spiritual capacity, is always

173

proving itself capable and worthy of so much better and higher ministry than he can give it. So the minister of the Gospel finds his own humility and the delightfulness of his work ever increasing together.

And this suggests one other point, which is the last that I shall speak of. I cannot but think that one of the truest ways in which Christianity has made humility at once a commoner and a nobler grace has been in the way in which it has furnished work for the higher powers of man, which used to be idle and only ponder proudly on themselves. Idleness standing in the midst of unattempted tasks is always proud. Work is always tending to humility. Work touches the keys of endless activity, opens the infinite, and stands awe-struck before the immensity of what there is to do. Work brings a man into the good realm of facts. Work takes the dreamy youth who is growing proud in his closet over one or two sprouting powers which he has discovered in himself, and sets him out among the gigantic needs and the vast processes of the world, and makes him feel his littleness. Work opens the measureless fields of knowledge and skill that reach far out of our sight. I am sure we all know the fine, calm, sober humbleness of men who have really tried themselves against the tasks of life. It was great in Paul, and in Luther, and in Cromwell. It is something that never comes into the character, never shows in the face of a man who has never worked. Is not this what you would do for a boy whom you saw getting proud, set him to work? He might be so poor of stuff that he would be proud of his work, poorly as he would do it. For the matter of that, men of poor stuff may be proud of anything, proud even of what they call their humility. But if he were really great enough to be humble at all, his work would bring him to humility.

174

He would be brought face to face with facts. He would measure himself against the eternal pillars of the universe. He would learn the blessed lesson of his own littleness in the way in which it is always learnt most blessedly, by learning the largeness of larger things. And all this, which the ordinary occupations of life do for our ordinary powers, Christianity, with the work that it furnishes for our affections and our hopes, does for the higher parts of us.

It is so easy for us to go through the motions of humility. It is—I will not say so hard—but it is so serious and so great a thing to be really humble. I have tried to show it to you as the consummate Christian grace; nay, rather as the star in the zenith, where all the sweep of Christian graces meets. Do you not see that it takes a whole Christian to be wholly humble? Christ came and plucked out of the depths of men's contempt this perfect quality and set it on the very summit of the hill of grace. I have tried to show you how He did it. He set men close to God, to their true selves, to the souls of their brethren, to the immensity of duty; and He said to them there, what there they understood, "Be humble!"

It was as if He took a proud, fretful man out of the worrying life of the selfish city and set him among the solemn mountains, and the mountains brought to him the blessed peace of humility and the sense of his own insignificance.

It seems to come to this, that Christianity is the religion of the broadest truthfulness. It does not set men at any work of mere resolution, saying, "Come, now, let us be humble." That would but multiply the endless specimens of useless self-mortification. But true Christianity puts men face to face with the humbling facts, the great realities, and

175

then humility comes upon the soul, as darkness comes on the face of the earth, not because the earth has made up its mind to be dark, but because it has rolled into the great shadow.

It is the narrowness of our life that makes us proud. I should think one of you merchants would be proud of his successful business if he saw nothing beyond it. I should think you men and women would be proud of your splendid houses if you look no farther. But if you could only see God forever present in your life, and Jesus dying for your soul, and your soul worth Jesus' dying for, and the souls of your brethren precious in His sight, and the whole universe teeming with work for Him, then must come the humility of the Christian. To that humility let us devote ourselves, for in a humility like that alone is peace.

✣

Pride and the Grace of God *

DONALD M. BAILLIE

"Not I, but the grace of God which was with me."
—1 Corinthians 15:10

IN ONE OF ROBERT LOUIS STEVENSON'S stories there is an incident which we may take as starting-point. Two men are standing together on the shore, beside a lagoon where pearl-fishing is being carried on, and on the beach in front of

---

*From *Out of Nazareth* by Donald M. Baillie, copyright 1958, Charles Scribner's Sons. Used by permission.

176

them lies a diving-costume. The sight of it sets one of them thinking and moralizing, and he makes a parable.

There is the diving-costume designed to cover a man from head to foot as he goes down into the water. It comes up out of the sea, dripping with water, and goes down again, and comes up again dripping with water, and all the while the man inside is untouched—as dry as if he had remained on land.

"Well," says the one man, "can't we imagine some spiritual kind of dress in which men could go out into the world, and amid all the disturbing and painful influences of life their hearts would remain safe and unharmed, like the man in the diving-costume? Can't we imagine such a dress for the soul?"

"Yes," says the second man, "it is called self-conceit."

"Oh," said the other, "why not call it the grace of God?"

It is a good parable. There are these two different kinds of armour by which different men contrive to keep themselves unhurt and so manage to go safely through all life's experiences. Some manage it by the armour of conceit, others by the armour of the grace of God. St. Paul managed it by the latter method. And that is precisely expressed in the words of our text, where St. Paul, speaking of his conversion to Christianity and his pioneering work for Christ, says, "Yet not I, but the grace of God which was with me."

St. Paul had a very adventurous life, with many difficult things to do, and many wounds to face. But the most difficult thing he ever had to do was when he had to face up to Christianity, which he had been persecuting, and admit that he had been utterly and dreadfully wrong, and turn round and begin all over again and become a Christian. That is what he has been talking of in these verses—how

177

he must be always the least of the apostles, because he was the last of them; he had been on the wrong side and then had come right, like one born out of due season.

How hard it must have been for his pride—or at least it would have been if he had tried to cling to his pride. He was such a well-known man, a learned man, a Pharisee, a brilliant young fellow, so sure of his convictions, and the pride of his sect. When he was confronted with this new movement called Christianity, it was a great shock—he had to make up his mind about it, and he made up his mind against it and tried to stamp it out. But somehow he couldn't get away from it—it continued to prick his conscience.

If he had determined to stick to his pride, he might have remained a Pharisee to the end of his days, protected against this new disturbing influence by the armour of conceit. But Paul couldn't do that, and so there came the great day on the Damascus road, when Paul had a vision of Christ, and threw his pride to the winds, and turned his back on all he had lived for, and began again at the very beginning as a Christian. And not a sad ashamed kind of Christian either, with pride fallen and conceit broken, and therefore going softly for the rest of his days. No, but a keen bold ardent adventurous enterprising Christian, always in the forefront of the battle, and with head erect, in spite of his long mistake. It was because he had given up the armour of conceit for the armour of the grace of God.

So in this place, after talking of himself as the least and last of the apostles, he goes on quite serenely. "But by the grace of God I am what I am. And his grace bestowed on me was not in vain, for I laboured more abundantly than

178

all of them. Yet not I, but the grace of God which was with me." Not conceit, but the grace of God.

Let us look at those two different kinds of armour.

(1) *The armour of conceit.* Why was it that, while Paul the Pharisee became a Christian, so many other Pharisees remained where they were, high and dry, uninfluenced by Christianity, untouched, unwounded, unblessed? Wasn't it because they were encased in the armour of conceit? That was what kept them safe. Not all of them, surely. It wouldn't be fair to condemn all of them in that way. But many of them—many of the Pharisees whom Jesus encountered. Wasn't that one of the things He saw in them —pride, self-righteousness, self-esteem? They were encased in that armour. When Jesus appeared among them, with His message and His challenge, that was something new and disturbing. And they couldn't bear to be disturbed. They didn't want new truth to upset their little system of things. They didn't want the challenge of a new ethic. They didn't want to have to change their minds about anything, or to be brought to repentance for anything, or to make new resolutions about anything. So they kept themselves safe, high and dry, within their armour of conceit and complacence (like the man in the diving-costume), and nothing could get through it. It kept them safe, sure enough; but it was a deadly kind of safety, for it meant that they never learnt anything, and they got nothing from Christ.

It is quite a common thing still for people to wear the unwholesome kind of armour as they go about the world. For example, there are people who learn very little as they go about the world because they are too proud to admit that they don't know. I dare say most of us are tempted

179

in that direction. We are sometimes too proud to ask questions. Children will always ask them, but we outgrow that, and we pretend to know, and so we don't learn anything like as much as we might. The armour of pride keeps us from learning.

Again, it keeps us from apprehending new truth, even in the deepest things. A great many minds are prejudiced against anything new and unfamiliar in religion, any new truth that sounds a little bit unorthodox or upsetting. And very often that is just the same armour of complacence and conceit—we won't believe we were wrong, we won't stretch our minds to consider anything new. In that way we often keep truth away from our minds, and it isn't good for us.

But above all, the armour of conceit keeps us from becoming better men and women. It keeps away the grace of God; grace and pride simply don't go together. The Bible tells us that "God resisteth the proud, but giveth grace unto the humble." Pride saves us no doubt from many humbling experiences, but thereby it keeps us from all moral and spiritual blessings.

In our Christian religion we talk a great deal about contrition and repentance and forgiveness and new beginnings; but very often we don't really give ourselves to these experiences. We are too proud. We don't want to be rebuked. We are not going to have ourselves continually upset. As we go about this world we would receive a good many hard knocks, and often find ourselves in the wrong, and frequently be made ashamed and have to acknowledge our shortcomings—if we were to allow ourselves to be touched and wounded in that way. But very often we won't. We are too proud. We encase ourselves in the armour of

180

pride—we will see our neighbour's faults but not our own. That saves us the pains of penitence. But it is at a terrible cost. For it keeps us time after time from making a new start. It keeps us from turning our back on the past and becoming better men and women. It is not a good thing to keep ourselves safely encased in the armour of conceit.

(2) *The armour of the grace of God.* "Not I," said Paul, "but the grace of God which was with me." I believe that when Paul became a Christian he began to think far less about himself than he had been accustomed to do, and far more about God; far less about his own character and achievements, and far more about what God was giving him and doing for him. The result was that his own character began to grow far finer than ever and his achievements became far greater than ever. And he knew it. But he wasn't a bit conceited or complacent about it, because he would always say: "Not I, but the grace of God which was with me." And I am sure that is the secret of the Christian life and of that marvellous thing which we call the Christian character.

It has often been pointed out that the Christian character is full of the strangest contradictions; it is an extraordinary combination of apparently opposite qualities: strength and tenderness, the wisdom of the serpent and the harmlessness of the dove, pessimism and optimism, solemnity and joy; but above all, humility and confidence. What explains it? How can a man be both perfectly humble and perfectly confident? It is, of course, because he is aways saying, consciously or unconsciously: "Not I, but the grace of God."

Here is a man faced with big responsibilities, a difficult enterprise, which seems beyond his powers of mind and will.

He tackles it, without undue worry. He makes mistakes, perhaps big ones. But that doesn't make him give it up. Why not? Is it because he is conceited and won't see and admit his mistakes? Well, if that is the kind of man he is, the armour of conceit will indeed keep his pride from being wounded. But he won't be a success. He'll be a failure, because he will never learn from his mistakes. But if he is a real Christian, he will see his mistakes. He will admit them and regret them. But he won't give it all up because of them. He won't be wounded unto death. He has an armour to save him from that—not the armour of conceit, but the armour of God's grace.

All along he hasn't been thinking of himself, his own cleverness, his own prestige, but of God, who set him where he is and gave him his task to perform. And so he will try again, stronger and wiser than ever. And in the long run he will prove equal to his responsibilities, and yet won't be conceited about it, because it is "Not I, but the grace of God."

Again (and this is a still more vital and central case) here is a man who time after time, every week that he lives, every day that he lives, acknowledges and confesses his sins. Isn't it a wonder that he doesn't give up the business of Christian living altogether? He would, if he had nothing better for his defence than the armour of conceit. For the armour couldn't stand it, and a man would soon, with the bitterness of fallen pride, give it up as a bad job. What's the good of trying to go on, when every day, in spite of our repentances, we fall short again, and lose our tempers, or say something cruel or mean, or play the coward, or do some other little thing that makes us feel ashamed? What's the good of it?

If you want to know the Christian answer to that question, here it is: Don't think so much of yourself. Think of God. Don't think just of your own character stained again. Think of God—His will disobeyed, His love wounded, and nevertheless His grace still waiting for you, ready to accept you again. Think of Him.

That is the one thing that always makes it worth while to go on, to begin again, to rise up out of penitence into new hope, because God is willing to forgive you, and the great reality with which you have to do is not just yourself, your character, your merits—not you, but the grace of God.

Friends, I believe that is the very heart of the Gospel of Christ and the secret of living victoriously amid all the difficulties and vicissitudes of the world. The word "grace" sounds mysterious (does it?)—just a bit of antiquated theological jargon. "The grace of God"—what does that mean? And what has it got to do with the life of a practical hard-headed man or woman in this modern world?

I reply "Everything." I am sure that the really practical people, the really effective people, the really admirable and enviable people, are the people who have exchanged the armour of self-righteousness for the armour of the grace of God.

From Childishness to Maturity

❀ ❀ ❀

In the midst of many other exhortations to the people at Philippi, Paul included this sentence, "Let those of us who are mature be thus minded" (Phil 3:15).

By the very nature of the statement it is evident he recognized that there is a difference between being mature in years and being mature in mind. Maturity in the emotional and spiritual sense has little to do with age. The law concerns itself with chronological age. When a person is twenty-one he can vote, sign contracts, and get married. He is considered mature. Everyone knows there are many people eligible to vote who are emotionally and spiritually immature. They are still meeting adult situations with the behavior responses of a child. They may be adults in many respects but still possess only the religion of a child.

In essence, the pastor today is striving for the same goals that Paul was seeking in his day. Only a mature response to life is adequate. In the famous thirteenth chapter of 1 Corinthians Paul said, "When I was a child, I spoke like a child, I thought like a child, I reasoned like a child; when I became a man, I gave up childish ways" (verse 11).

To move from childishness to maturity involves many kinds of growth. It means one should grow out of childish egocentricity and recognize the needs and feelings of others. It means one should be able to accept responsibility, to recognize one's own place in the home and in society. It means one should develop the capacity to face difficulty and discouragement without whimpering or complaining. It means one should attain a scale of values, have some convictions about those things that are of real worth, be able to make choices, and work for future goals.

Religiously it means one has increased both in his understanding of his faith and in his experiences of faith. The child accepts the religion of his parents, his family, his minister. As he becomes an adult, he must grapple with this religion and live by its teachings until it becomes his own.

This is not done once and for all. Maturity of both mind and spirit is a matter of constant growth. Sometimes the pastor works with an individual as he struggles to grow; at other times the pastor preaches to a group of individuals assembled in worship, helping them all to grow.

(1) Through preaching the pastor can present the biblical concept of a mature religion as a guide and challenge to all.

(2) Through preaching the pastor can point out the inadequacy of an immature response to life and can help his parishioners "give up childish ways."

(3) Through preaching the pastor can aid in the continued growth necessary for all maturity. Just as maturity of body comes as a result of continued growth, so does maturity of soul, but only to those who fulfill the conditions. Through preaching the pastor can help people fulfill the conditions through which growth takes place.

(4) Through preaching the pastor can present the ideal toward which all men can strive so that they may "attain to the unity of the faith and of the knowledge of the Son of God, to mature manhood, to the measure of the stature of the fullness of Christ" (Eph. 4:13).

❊

I'd Grow Up *

CLOVIS G. CHAPPELL

"I put away childish things."—1 Corinthians 13:11

PAUL IS HERE making a tremendous assertion. He does not claim that he has put away the childlike. To do that would not be triumph but tragedy. He claims that he has put away the childish. As he has come to physical maturity, so he has reached some degree of mental and spiritual maturity. A little baby is a beautiful creature that excites our love and expectation. The coming of a seven-pound baby into a home is something to make the heart sing. But suppose the baby, instead of weighing seven pounds, should weigh 150. That would not make for laughter, but for tears. In fact, the infancy of the grownup is one of life's crowning tragedies.

I

"I put away childish things." What are these childish things? There are certain characteristics that mark us as childish regardless of our age.

1. Little children are much given to tears. We expect them to weep more or less, therefore their wails do not greatly upset us. Not only do babies weep, but they weep over trifles as well as over things that really matter. It does

---

not take a deadly wound to make them cry out. A slight pin scratch will serve just as well. They howl at a touch of colic, or if dinner is a few minutes late. There is nothing too small to upset their little world and cause them to yell at the top of their lungs.

Not only are babies easily moved to tears, but their crying is always over some personal calamity. What those about them may be suffering matters nothing. The slightest pain upsets them far more than an earthquake in a neighboring city or even a world war. They weep easily but always for themselves. Never do they have a tear for the woes and wants of others.

2. A second characteristic of the infant is his love of attention. He must have the center of the stage. That is one reason he cries. When he grows a bit older, that is the reason he displays his sore toe. That is the reason, when he grows older still, that he tells you how badly life has treated him, that he gives you a blow-by-blow description of what his nerves are doing, that he informs you of his operation and ends by fervently hoping that you will never have to suffer as he has suffered.

Sometimes his love of attention takes another direction. He is willing to work, but only when he is in the lead. He is willing to play, but only when he chooses the game. If he is voted down, he refuses to be a good democrat. Instead, he sulks in his tent and goes no more to battle. He washes his hands of the whole business, declaring emphatically, "My way is right. I am always right, and if you don't do my way then I am through."

There is no measuring the harm that such big babies work in the ordinary business of living. They can be terribly in the way in the church. Often they can wreck a home. Some time ago I married a young couple, one of whom had not grown up. When the wife did something that displeased this big baby, instead of talking it over with her, he puffed up and pouted and had her guessing at what was wrong. Sometimes it is the other way round. The husband goes to work and forgets to kiss his wife good-by, or he fails to remember an anniversary. Then when he comes home at night, she looks like a chronic pain. When he asks an explanation, she refuses to give it. Such people are too childish to make a success out of the big adventure of marriage.

Then often we show our childishness by demanding appreciation. Of course, everybody loves appreciation. It is far harder to carry on when nobody approves. But to fail to do so is not a mark of maturity but of the opposite. The baby produces a bit of a sensation when he takes his first step. Everybody gathers about to applaud. But if the child expects that applause to continue throughout life, he is likely to be disappointed. If he reaches the place where he refuses to walk without it, then it means he has never grown up. The childish must have attention. They like the center of the stage. Some even commit crimes just to see their names in the paper.

3. A third mark of childishness is the taking of life's blessings as a matter of course. Accepting them as their deserts, babies naturally have no sense of gratitude. You may trot a colicky baby on your knees for half the night, but he will never show the slightest appreciation. When did ever a baby look into a tired mother's eyes and say, "Thank you"? We can take such ingratitude from little babies, but from big ones it is far harder to bear. There are

188

few uglier signs of perpetual infancy than never to learn to say either to God or man, "I thank you."

4. A fourth mark of infancy is to have no sense of obligation. Whenever a child begins to want to give back something for what he has received, we are encouraged. That means that he is growing. But there are those in whom a sense of obligation never develops. They are always thinking in terms of what the world owes them, never in terms of what they owe the world. Some time ago I saw a frail-looking mother walking down the street with an unusually husky youngster. This vigorous lad walked along beside her for a little while. Then he decided that he would ride. So he began to demand that his mother carry him. She sought to reason with him, tried to tell him how weary she was. But his only answer was to run in front of her, seize her around the knees, and stop her in her tracks. Then she took the giant into her arms, and I did not know which one needed the woodshed the more. Such clamoring to be carried is bad even in a lad of three, but in one of forty it is utterly hideous.

5. Finally, childish folks are selfish. All small children are self-centered. The fact that they wail over their own petty disappointments and over theirs only, their demand for attention, their lack of a sense of gratitude and of obligation, all these are but the streams that flow from the fountain of self-centeredness. Selfishness is never winsome. Old people may be very ugly or they may be very beautiful. When they are ugly, their crowning ugliness, generally speaking, is born of the fact that they have become childish.

Years ago I was invited to dine in a certain home of whose tragedy I was entirely ignorant. Therefore, you can imagine some of my amazement, upon my arrival at that home, when I saw a man fully six feet in height playing about on the lawn clad in a checked apron of the style that he wore when he was two or three years of age. More than a score of years before a baby had gladdened that home. But the sunshine that he had brought had now changed into the blackest of shadows. This was the case because, though he had grown in body, he had never grown in mind and heart. His was the tragedy of perpetual infancy. To refuse to put away childish things is to become a grief to both God and man.

II

Not only did Paul put away childish things, but for his immaturity he substituted maturity. What are some of the marks of maturity? What is there about Paul that indicates that he has really become a man?

1. The fact that Paul has grown up does not mean that he has put away tears altogether. He still weeps, but he no longer weeps over petty trifles. Nor are his tears shed simply for troubles personal to himself. He can, of course, still weep over his own sorrows. Our Lord does not call upon us to hate ourselves and to love our neighbors. He calls upon us to love our neighbors as we love ourselves. But while Paul still weeps, his tears are now almost wholly for others. "Ye know," he writes, "from the first day that I came into Asia, after what manner I have been with you at all seasons, serving the Lord with all humility of mind, and with many tears, and temptations, which befell me by the lying in wait of the Jews." His tears are like the tears of his Master. They are born of his heartache for others.

190

They indicate that self has died under the stroke of the Cross, and that he has truly learned to rejoice with those that do rejoice and to weep with those that weep.

2. Paul can now carry on when nobody applauds. This does not mean that he does not care for the approval of his fellows. Every sensitive soul longs for such approval. But it does mean that if this approval is withheld, he does not give over and quit. "I will very gladly," he writes, "spend and be spent for you, though the more abundantly I love you the less I be loved." He has not only reached the place where he can carry on when nobody applauds, but even when folks ignore or disapprove, or become positively antagonistic. That is a mark of maturity.

3. The fact that Paul has grown up is further indicated by his deep sense of gratitude. In truth, that is one of his most beautiful characteristics. As we follow his eventful life, we find him in all sorts of trying and perplexing situations. Sometimes he is at the whipping post, sometimes in personal danger, sometimes he is putting through difficult tasks with no human backing. Again we find him in prison without his beloved books and without even a coat to keep him warm. But we never find him without his song of gratitude. "In everything," he writes, "give thanks." That has become the habit of his life. Blessed is the man who has so attained. I know no surer mark of maturity than a constant gratitude that grows out of our realization that we have nothing that we have not received either from God or from our fellows.

4. Finally, Paul indicates that he has become of age by his deep sense of obligation. "I am debtor," he writes. Having received so much and so persistently, he feels that he is under vast obligations to serve. Such a sense of obliga-

tion is always a mark of maturity. To be utterly lacking in it is always to remain an infant.

When the ancient Greeks sought to teach this lesson, they told how, when Achilles was born, his mother consulted the oracle to inquire as to the future of her son. That oracle told her that Achilles would either live a short life of battle and of victory or a long life of inglorious ease. Being a mother, and a mistaken mother at that, she chose the latter course. Therefore, she dressed him like a girl and hid him on an island where nobody lived but girls. He looked like a girl, played like a girl, and everybody thought he was a girl.

Then came the war against Troy. When the Greeks consulted the oracle as to how they might win, they were told that they could never win without Achilles. But nobody knew where Achilles was. Therefore, Ulysses set out to find him. At last he came to the island where nobody lived but girls. He disguised himself as a peddler. He filled his pack with the trinkets and toys that girls love, but underneath he put a sword and a suit of shining armor. When he reached the island and displayed his wares, the girls bought eagerly. But one girl looked on with indifference, even contempt. Then Ulysses displayed the sword and the armor. At once the indifferent girl became all eagerness. She seized the sword and wielded it. She fitted on the armor. "Here," cried Ulysses, "is our hero!" He recognized him because he chose weapons instead of toys. In thus choosing he showed a sense of obligation.

But to have no sense of oughtness is always to remain a child. Children love to play. That is all to the good. For them playing is an end in itself. As we grow older, we ought still to play. We cannot render our best service without it. But with grownups playing must be a means to an end rather than an end in itself. There are many names by which I would not like to be called. There are few that I would hate more than this—"Playboy." To have come and grown and gone and never to have felt the hand of compulsion laid upon me, never to have said with my Master, "I must!"—that is about as damning a sin as one can commit.

III

Now how did Paul become a man? He did not do so by pulling up all the childish weeds in the garden of his soul one by one. No more did he change from moral and spiritual infancy into maturity in an instant. There was no magic about his coming to manhood. How, I repeat, did it come about? It was not instantaneous, it was a process. Paul became a man by growing.

Growth is an amazing miracle. No wonder Thomas Carlyle, holding a baby in his arms, looked at it with eyes of wonder. "Just to think," he said, "that Shakespeare was once like this!" And so he was! So was Hitler! So was Mussolini! So was Paul! So even was Jesus! When Luke undertakes to tell us how Jesus became the perfect Man that he was, he tells us that it was because he grew in the right direction. "Jesus increased in wisdom and stature, and in favor with God and man."

Seeing that Paul became mature by growth, how did he grow? How may you and I grow? It may help us to realize that growth under proper conditions is the most natural thing in the world. We do not grow by merely spitting on our hands. We do not grow by saying, "Go to, now! I am going to cease to be small and become large." Growth is a law of life. We grow, not by trying, but by meeting the conditions of growth. Here, for instance, is a normal, healthful baby. How does that baby grow? Not by worrying about it. He grows naturally, spontaneously, unconsciously, as he meets certain conditions. What are those conditions?

1. He eats. In fact, he seems little more than an appetite. If he fails to eat, he not only fails to grow but he dies. As food is necessary for the baby, so it is for you and me if we are to reach the kind of Christian manhood that was experienced by Paul. Why do so many who unite with the Church fail to make any progress? Why are they so often no bigger at the end of the day than they were at the beginning? For multitudes this is the answer: They fail to get the right kind of food. They make little or nothing of prayer. They seldom look into God's Word. Thus they do not give themselves a chance to feed on the Bread of Life. One might as well expect to become a strong athlete by feeding on wind as to become a mature Christian by feeding on a diet that has in it no food for either mind or heart.

Some years ago a small group of scientists got lost in the wilds of Australia. They ran out of food. In their extremity they found the root of a certain plant that was palatable. But, though they ate of this heartily, they died to a man. When their bodies were found and the contents of their stomachs tested, it was found that the root they had been eating was absolutely devoid of food value. Such is the case with the diet upon which many professing Christians are trying to feed themselves today. They are careful about vitamins for the body while the diet upon which they seek to feed their minds would not contain a vitamin to the carload.

2. A healthy baby grows not only by eating but by exercise. A good bit of his yelling is nature's way of developing his lungs. When he kicks and tries to swallow now his foot and now his fist, he is taking his daily dozen. He is giving himself a workout. As exercise is necessary for a growing baby, so it is for a growing Christian. The low state of health of many church people may be explained by the fact that they never take any exercise.

Let me speak this personal word to you who have come to question the reality of religion. Have you found in your Christian experience more of weight than of wings? Has God become as vague for you as a dream? Then go out today and take a little exercise by serving others. Jesus declared, "For the Son of man is come to seek and to save that which is lost." Set yourself for a single day on that same mission and see what happens. It is perfectly marvelous how doubt melts in the warmth of an effort to do some good in the world. Growth is sure and natural when we eat the right kind of food and take the right kind of exercise.

3. Finally, the baby, having eaten and taken his daily dozen, goes to sleep. If we are to grow, we need not only food and exercise but rest as well. I am not now speaking mainly of rest for the body, though that is essential. Only this week I had a communication from an old school friend who has had to give up his work. He explained his breakdown in these words: "I have run past too many stop lights." Physical rest is good and essential. The man who works hard and fails to rest is sinning against God and his own body.

But the rest of which I am thinking now is that inward rest that Jesus promised when he walked among men. It is the rest that he promises now. Today, as in the long ago, he is saying to you and to me: "Come unto me, all ye that labor and are heavy laden, and I will give you rest. Take my yoke upon you, and learn of me; for I am meek and lowly in heart: and ye shall find rest unto your souls." Accept this invitation wholeheartedly, and you will know the gladness of growth. More and more you will experience one of the chief joys both of the life that now is and of that which is to come, the joy of growing. "Beloved, now are we the sons of God, and it doth not yet appear what we shall be: but we know that, when he shall appear, we shall be like him; for we shall see him as he is." Surely one of the richest privileges both of time and of eternity is the privilege of growing more and more into the likeness of our blessed Lord!

✻

The Struggle for Maturity *

WAYNE E. OATES

When I was a child, I spoke like a child, I thought like a child, I reasoned like a child; when I became a man, I gave up childish ways.

—1 Cor. 13:11

Therefore let us leave the elementary doctrines of Christ and go on to maturity, not laying again a foundation of repentance from dead works and of

---

*Reprinted from *The Revelation of God in Human Suffering* by Wayne Oates. © 1959, W. L. Jenkins. The Westminster Press. Used by permission.

faith toward God, with instruction about ablutions, the laying on of hands, the resurrection of the dead, and eternal judgment.—Heb. 6:1-2

Rather, speaking the truth in love, we are to grow up in every way into him who is the head, into Christ, from whom the whole body, joined and knit together by every joint with which it is supplied, when each part is working properly, makes bodily growth and upbuilds itself in love.
—Eph. 4:15-16

THE STRUGGLE FOR MATURITY entails more suffering than do most of our momentary afflictions. Our capacity to learn from them, to discern the workings of the mind of God in stress situations, and to lay hold of the maturing resources of God's grace in these momentary situations largely depends upon our accrued maturity in Christ. The struggle for maturity is, at the heart of its meaning, the thrust of the total person in the ceaselessly changing and growing experience of relating oneself abidingly to other people and to God. The process of building mature relationships to God and to our community is another way of saying that through the divine gift of God's love we are initially enabled *to begin* to participate in the Kingdom of God. God lays the foundation of the building of mature relationships to himself and others by first having loved us in Jesus Christ our Lord. He touches us in our infirmities and quickens us in our incapacities; he perceives our low estimates of ourselves and discerns the impediments of our character that hinder us from loving him and one another with abandon and wholehearted passion, unsullied by lust. Mature relationships do not come to pass by lifting ourselves by the bootstraps of self-effort. Mature relationships are activated out of the heart of God himself in that he valued us in a way we could never have valued ourselves: he so loved us that he gave himself for us.

The love of God as the beginning and end of mature relationships is set forth in the thirteenth chapter of First Corinthians. Here the perfect love of God, the necessity for mature relationships to God and to one another, and the different kinds of immaturity among growing Christians are all set forth.

First, let us look at the different kinds of immaturity among growing Christians. Secondly, the supreme criterion of spiritual maturity, love, as the heart of interpersonal relationships needs consideration. Finally, the practical ways in which this maturity expresses itself in interpersonal living will be given attention.

The Christian, having encountered the love of God and having entered the Christian life, is, nevertheless, still involved in spiritual immaturities of various kinds. The "if's" of 1 Cor. 13:1-3 depict four types of spiritual immaturity.

Spiritual Articulation

The first immaturity is that stage of spiritual growth which I choose to call *the articulation and explanation of the remarkable change that has occurred in one's inner being*. The early Christians, like many of us, were in many instances uneducated and unlettered persons when they entered the Christian life. They could not find words to describe their feelings. The message of the new being in Christ burned within them and sought expression in words lest it consume them with its intensity. Some of them were so overcome with its power that they could only babble like an infant. They burst forth in unknown tongues, with no language but a cry. Yet those who also had become Christians could understand through subverbal communication that which their spiritual kinsmen were trying to utter. Paul cautioned his converts, however, to work at the business of making themselves clearly understood, lest outsiders and unbelievers consider them mad. Five words with a clear understanding are more instructive than ten thousand words in a tongue. (1 Cor. 14:24 and 19, respectively.)

Men like Apollos were eloquent and spoke with much smoothness and power of oratory. Paul saw "cliques" of Christians go off after Apollos, and was quite aware of the fact that he himself did not speak in "lofty words of wisdom" (1 Cor. 2:1). He saw that many of the Corinthian Christians had become fixated at this level of spiritual maturity and had become involved in speaking "in the tongues of men and of angels." As they became so fixated, they were more and more immature as time went on.

Even so, you and I get the impression too often that the person who can *say* his gospel most beautifully is *therefore* the most mature. We tend to judge ourselves and others by our ability to speak of the gospel.

Now speech is the life line of our communication with one another. It is here that counseling and healing begin: in the articulation of feeling and communication. We must, therefore, never cease to work at the business of devising ways of making ourselves understood to one another. Much of our irritability, our impatience, our rudeness, and our rejoicing when others go wrong comes of our plain inability to make ourselves understood to others. Our stubborn unwillingness to discipline ourselves to hear what they have to say leads to confused relationships. Rather, we are thinking up what we are going to say instead of listening to them as they talk.

However, our most profound communication is deeper than words and consists of those "groanings of the spirit which cannot be uttered." Just *telling* their troubles does not necessarily make people whole. Communication must itself grow apace with the development of our capacity to love. "Even if we speak in the tongues of men and of angels, and have not this, we are as a noisy gong or a clanging cymbal." We have not matured in our love if we stop here in our growth. If many of us like this get together, we may develop a "tin-pan alley" religious cult.

Spiritual Understanding

The development of insight and understanding, knowledge, and the sense of mystery is a second type of immaturity. To the psychologically sophisticated, this sounds strange, because we tend to equate insight and maturity. But it is only a second way station in the pilgrimage to maturity. The more we try to communicate our experience as Christians, the more it is necessary for us to develop insight and understanding of ourselves and others. We learn how to be self-aware without being self-conscious and uneasy. We learn how to understand our own motivations and those of others without letting our understanding become a tool for our power to condemn ourselves and others. We learn how to be prophetic for the whole mind of God. We learn how to participate in the mysterious presence and ineffable knowledge of God without becoming a cultist or a spiritually arrogant individual.

Paul confronted persons among the Corinthians who had lost their balance on these important issues. He confronted the Greek philosophers who had "all knowledge" and often wanted it known. He also confronted the worshipers of the mystery cults of the day. He had to warn his followers of false prophets who had come among them. These persons permitted their systems of faith, organizations of knowledge, and particular "in-group" relationships to a few people to cut them off and isolate them from the larger Christian community. Apart from the power of love in interpersonal relationships, even knowledge itself becomes a divisive factor.

The reality of these truths is at every hand in the academic world of colleges and universities, seminaries, and divinity schools today. As Robert Frost says in his poem "The Cabin in the Clearing," we live "in the fond faith accumulated fact will of itself take fire and light the world up." As T. S. Eliot has aptly said:

Where is the wisdom we have lost in knowledge?
Where is the knowledge we have lost in information?

(From "Choruses from 'The Rock'" by T. S. Eliot, *Collected Poems 1909-1962;* Harcourt, Brace & World, Inc. Reprinted by permission.)

Likewise, analytically oriented persons are likely to stop growing at the very point of delving for more and more subtle and occult interpretations of their own motives. Having been given the power to love, they may stop at futile speculation! If we stop in the pilgrimage of our spiritual lives at this plateau, we have not moved to the highest level of maturity in building our relationships to God and others. We must move on. This is no stopping place, only a rest along the way.

The Moving Power Of Faith

A third kind of immaturity suggested by Paul is an overdependence upon a "moving" faith, demonstrating its power. Overwhelmed by the inadequacy of our knowledge, that is, that we know in part and prophesy in part, we move upward to realize that we live by faith. We begin to "trust in the Lord with all our hearts and lean not on our own understanding." We may even tend to disparage the value of human knowledge and to decry the efforts of science. We may even discount these realities to such an extent as to set science and religion over against each other. Instead of becoming a minister of reconciliation, we may turn into an apostle of discord. Pushed by our immaturity at this point, we may feel compelled to demonstrate the power of faith, that is, that it can move mountains, help people to get well without the aid of doctors, and solve our economic distress without the necessity of work, and so on. These signs of immaturity were on hand when Paul ministered to the Corinthians, and the timelessness of his truth is obvious in that they are still to be seen in the realm of those who profess themselves to be the most powerful in faith above all others. Likewise, persons who have been in deeper analysis and psychotherapy may avoid adult decisions and impossible action by extolling the virtues of their analyst, of analysis, and of its necessity for "every living creature."

202

But even here in the demonstration of faith above all others, we can easily see that such "uses" of faith and therapy divide people from one another rather than nurture them in sustaining relationships of love. Paul, in another place (Gal. 5:6), says that "faith works through love." In the thirteenth chapter of First Corinthians, he tells us that he is as nothing in spiritual apprehension and maturity as long as he uses his faith as a means of gain, that is, to demonstrate his personal prowess.

The Peril Of Activism

A fourth type of spiritual immaturity which we encounter on our pilgrimage toward maturity is seen in our attempts to express our faith through a vocation. Here we center down on becoming proficient in our work. We become activists who are set to a task and not to be deterred from it. This is good, but it is both our hope and our destruction. Our hope is here because it means that we have a sense of responsibility that motivates us to effective action. Our destruction is here because here lies our capacity to deceive ourselves into believing that the way to relate ourselves to God is by the sheer results of our work achievements.

We burn the candle at both ends, we "rack up" our successes, we carefully record our achievements, we remind others of our most recent honors and we keep our right hand informed of what our left hand is doing at all times. Yet the inner gnawing of anxiety tells us that we are missing the main point of living and that we have gained nothing in reality. We have missed the power of the joy that comes to us by having taken the time to establish enduring and satisfying relationships to people and to inquire in the temple of the Lord how we may know and love him better. T. S. Eliot again helps us when he says

What life have you if you have not life together?
There is no life that is not in community,
And no community not lived in praise of God. . . .
And now you live dispersed on ribbon roads,
And no man knows or cares who is his neighbour
Unless his neighbour makes too much disturbance,
But all dash to and fro in motor cars,
Familiar with the roads and settled nowhere. . . .
And the wind shall say: "Here were decent godless
    people:
Their only monument the asphalt road
And a thousand lost golf balls."

(From "Choruses from 'The Rock' " from *Collected Poems 1909-1962* by T. S. Eliot; Harcourt, Brace & World, Inc. Reprinted by permission.)

This is very descriptive of the person today who enters a profession and whose profession *becomes* his religion. He gives up his "body to be burned" in activistic achievement. This is his religion. He may be a doctor, a minister, a social worker, a lawyer, a psychologist, or a scientist in the physical sciences. He reaches the age of thirty-five or forty with a breathless anxiety, burned up with ambition, eaten out with tension, and fearfully apprehensive of his health. He may have the "success syndrome" of ulcers, heart pains, fatigue, confusion, and an inner sense of emptiness, meaninglessness, and boredom. He is a stranger to his family and at cross purposes with his fellow workers,

204

and he feels that he is in a far country, far from God.

All four of these types of immaturity are really way stations along the path toward spiritual maturity in relationship to God and others. They point in the direction of maturity only when we make the supreme criterion of maturity—*agapē,* Christian love—our aim. When we reach this realization, then speaking "in the tongues of men and of angels," developing "prophetic powers" and a moving faith, achieving knowledge and insight, and giving up our bodies to be burned in activistic competition—all these appear as childish things, and at best as ways of establishing relationships of love to God and our fellow man.

The Full-Grownness of Love

Therefore, we need to arrive at an understanding of the meaning of love in terms of our maturity in relationship to God and others. In a word, without Christian love, all our other efforts at maturity thrust us into an encounter with nothingness, embroil us in futility, and make of life an empty meaninglessness that threatens our very being. We become as nothing.

Martin Buber gives a concept of interpersonal relationships in his book *I and Thou,* whereby we may think in a straight line about the true maturity in relationship to God and others. He says that there are two kinds of relationships to God and others. The first relationship is the I-It relationship, in which we "use" God and others to achieve our own chosen ends, apart from a freehearted participation on the part of God and others in our choosing of the ends we would achieve. Such a relationship treats people as things and God as an occult power for our own manipulation. It is characterized by an *extractive* kind of relatedness whereby we "get out" of people what we want, develop hostile relationships to them, and then "no longer have any use for them." As we often say about people whom we do not like—or better, whom we cannot dominate, use, or manipulate—"we don't have a bit of *use* for them." Naturally, the very image of God within other persons rises up in rebellion at the tyranny of such exploitation, and a real break in interpersonal relationships occurs.

Prayer, which is the name we give to our interpersonal relationship to God, can be understood afresh from this point of view. Many persons relate themselves to God at one time or another in an I-It kind of prayer. God becomes a "purveyor to their own appetites," to use Browning's phrase, one who caters to their own chosen ends in life, ends that have been chosen without consulting or considering his creative plan for life. A fervent desire to achieve some chosen end becomes, for all practical purposes, a god, an idol, and the eternal God and Father of our Lord Jesus Christ becomes the servant of the idol—in our own deluded way of thinking, to say the least. As such, prayer becomes a type of magic, that is, the management of infinite powers by finite persons. This is particularly true in the search for health and financial success.

Buber suggests a second kind of relationship that is radically different from the I-It relationship. He calls it the I-Thou relationship. Here we relate ourselves to God and to one another as *persons,* and not as things. Persons are ends within themselves rather than means to ulterior ends. The content of the Christian meaning of love can be put into Buber's concept of the I-Thou relationship, thereby aiding in a vital discovery of the meaning of the prophetic conception of love that had its roots in Hebrew thinking. Love is the capacity to accept responsibility for others and to relate to them in terms of their essential rather than their instrumental value. People are more than sheep or cattle; they are more than mere measuring sticks for our own ego achievements; they are more than tools for us to exploit; they are essentially valuable in and of themselves as "persons for whom Christ died," as having been initially made in "the image of God."

Likewise, God is the chief end of our existence, not we the chief end of his being. We find our prayers filled with all the fullness of God when we glorify him rather than attempt to subvert him to our petty pursuits in life. Prayer becomes adoration, thanksgiving, participation in fellowship, and the transformation of our selfhood into the likeness of him more than mere petition and a childish whining after one toy of desire and another. These things are added unto us, not as the end intention, but as the "afterthought by-product" of God's already existing knowledge of our needs.

The practical outworking of such a relationship of mature love of God and others is obvious in the thinking of Paul.

We become more secure and can be freed more and more of our impatience and unkindness toward others. We can evaluate their misunderstandings of us in a new light: the light of our failure to communicate our real motives clearly and in the light of our "inhuman use of them as humans." We are not so watchful of self-comparisons, because our own status is built by their success. The necessity for arrogance and rudeness is nil in genuinely secure people who feel that they have been accepted and understood for what they are really worth: persons for whom Christ died. Such persons value one another so highly that there is no need that they build one another or themselves up through bragging and boasting. They can only rejoice in the success of others and be grieved by others' failures. The relationships of life become more enduring, and they "last on."

In the relationships of love, Jesus Christ is always breaking through in some new revelation of his love through persons' concern for one another. Mature Christians are always searching their relationships to others and testing their knowledge of God with others. They live in the constant hope that God will again make himself known to them in their breaking of bread with one another. Their speaking, their prophecy, their understanding, and their faith and works are all set into a new contextual meaning of the love of God. This love, made known to them in the abiding relationship of Christ to them in the new covenant of his blood, becomes their clear channel of interpersonal relationship to one another.

Through Discipline to Freedom

✤ ✤ ✤

In the introductory chapters we said that the preacher must preach to human needs. Some of these needs are felt needs; some are not. The conscientious pastor must deal with both.

One need that all men have, although not all are aware of it, is the need for discipline. Those who are very much aware of their lack of discipline may seek a pastor's help. Many times in counseling sessions a pastor will hear such statements as these: "I know I ought to study harder"; "I wish I could control my temper more"; "I guess I'm just lazy"; "God knows I don't want to be this way"; "I intended to be in church every Sunday"; "I wish I could live up to my good intentions"; "I just don't have any discipline." Such people sincerely want more discipline, and they deserve help.

There are others who do not realize that discipline is one of their basic needs. They need to be convinced of its value. William James used to say that most men don't live within sight of their possibilities. One reason many fall far short of their true potential is their lack of discipline. No one ever drifts into real achievement; no one ever attains knowledge, understanding, and skill or develops a vital, meaningful spiritual life without great effort and persistent pursuance of goals.

209

Discipline is the key. Why, then, is it not more frequently the subject of sermons? Perhaps one reason is that the word "discipline" has a negative connotation. It implies punishment, as when a child is disciplined in school. In fact, one definition in the dictionary is "to punish or penalize." The word also implies restriction, hard work, austerity. Freedom, people say, that is desirable, but not discipline.

The truth of the matter is that freedom comes through discipline. Work and restriction at times lead to freedom. Paderewski had complete freedom at the keyboard. He was a master at the piano. But he said, "Before I was a master, I was a slave."

In any area where great achievement has come, where someone has attained great freedom, whether it is in art, athletics, preaching, music, surgery, or anything else, it has come through discipline. Great skill, great knowledge, and inner confidence always come at a price after continued effort and, at times, drudgery. There is no attainment in any field without discipline.

This is true, for example, of spiritual attainment. John R. Mott was one of the truly great men of recent times. When reading of his accomplishments, one is amazed at what one man can achieve. Mott had great natural ability, to be sure, but more than ability is needed to explain his career. His biographer said he had "dedicated and disciplined every power of body, mind and spirit . . . through decade after decade, for the Kingdom of God."

Preaching about discipline can have exciting results. If the preacher can persuade one person to dedicate and discipline "every power of body, mind and spirit," no one can tell how far-reaching the results may be.

This is not something that applies only to geniuses like Paderewski or to men of five talents like John R. Mott. All the members of the congregation need self-discipline. It is the preacher's task to make them aware of this need, to give them a vision of possibilities, to challenge them to make the effort, to encourage them to persevere until they attain their full potential, until they move from dissatisfaction to fulfillment and from discipline to freedom.

(1) Through preaching the pastor can present the biblical challenge to a completely dedicated, committed life. "For the gate is narrow and the way is hard . . ." (Matt. 7:14).

(2) Through preaching the pastor can illustrate the truth that all great men have attained their freedom and their mastery through discipline.

(3) Through preaching the pastor can make his parishioners aware of possibilities of growth and achievement, and he can challenge them to renewed effort.

(4) Through preaching the pastor can encourage those who have tried and failed, or become discouraged to make new efforts, to persevere until they gain freedom.

The sermon which follows by Harry Emerson Fosdick was preached in the days prior to World War II, and the allusions in the sermon to the rise of dictators deal with problems of that day. However, the message as a whole is as pertinent and as needed today as then. Serenity, the subject of the sermon by Dr. Fosdick presented earlier in this book, may at first glance seem to contradict the subject of discipline, but if one reads both sermons, he will see that they are complementary.

The second sermon dealing with discipline is by James Reid and is entitled "The Place of Self-Discipline."

❧

The Return to Discipline *

HARRY EMERSON FOSDICK

OUR WORLD TODAY faces us with at least one elemental
necessity—the need of discipline. Mankind can stand all
sorts of evils, but it cannot long endure chaos, disorder,
anarchy. When that reaches a certain point reaction sets
in and some force rises to bring confusion under control
and whip things into shape. The major movements of our
time—communism, naziism, fascism, militarism, the growing elements of dictatorship in the democracies—are all
endeavors to get some kind of order out of chaos, to put a
bridle on this wild horse, to bring our nations and our
world under disciplined control. Give the devil his due!
The totalitarianism we fear today at home and abroad is
an endeavor to get some social order out of the anarchic
confusion of the world.

Willy nilly, therefore, we face a choice on which our
personal lives and our social fortunes depend. Either we
are going to have enough people who discipline themselves
from within, or else we are going to have discipline imposed
on us from without. From that dilemma there is no escape.
In any population, large or small, let chaotic disorder
reach too great proportions and the demand will rise, at all

*From *Living Under Tension* by Harry Emerson Fosdick. Copyright 1941 by
Harper & Brothers. Reprinted by permission of Harper & Row, Publishers.

costs, for order. Though it take a dictator, that will seem a small price to pay for social order. The worst thing that mankind can face is anarchy.

Now there are two ways in which men achieve ordered societies: either they discipline themselves within, or else they have discipline imposed on them from without. The first gives leeway for liberty, and makes democracy possible; the second is the nucleus of dictatorship. This morning, then, we try to measure the importance of self-discipline, not only as one secret in great personal living but as one of the most towering social necessities of our time. For look at the world, and see! In so far as we do not discipline ourselves, someone else will impose discipline on us.

Self-control has not been characteristic of our generation. Have we in this country been a disciplined people? In our personal morals, in our respect for law, in our family life, in our subjugation of self-interest to the common welfare, in any regard that you can think of have we been a self-controlled people? We have had splendid virtues—energy, vigor, pioneering venturesomeness—explosive and aggressive virtues that could blast new roads through high mountains, and win for us what we call success. But winning that, how often has liberty turned to license, self-restraint been thrown to the winds, laxness rather than self-control characterized us! How often has our use of power, like a wayward stream at flood, burst its banks, and our personal lives been undedicated and uncontrolled! Well, America faces now one of the most fateful hours in its history, and no saying of Jesus, I think, is more pertinent to our need than this: "Wide is the gate, and broad is the way, that leadeth to destruction, and many are they that enter in thereby. For narrow is the gate, and

213

straitened the way, that leadeth unto life, and few are they that find it." So! The loose life means ruin; only the disciplined life can be great.

Nevertheless, deep in human nature are moods and attitudes that resist this truth, so that we may well organize our thought this morning by listening as, one by one, these moods rise up in protest against it.

First of all, who does not feel within himself the mood that cries, I want a rich, free life; I resent restraint and control—that is not the end of existence; copious, plenteous, bountiful living is what I want? Confronting that mood is the fact that abundant life and how to get it was what Jesus was talking about. He said that a loose, sprawling, meandering course never reaches it, only the narrow gate and the straitened way of a disciplined and dedicated life.

The other day I heard Kreisler and the Philharmonic Orchestra play Beethoven's *Concerto in D Major*. It was glorious. He never arrived at the fullness of artistic power and life by traveling a broad, meandering course. He began playing the violin when he was a small boy, not too promising. When he was fourteen he toured the United States, only moderately successful, so that, returning to Vienna he could not get a position as a second violinist in the Philharmonic there. He dropped the violin, therefore, thinking he was a failure at it; tried medicine, did not like it; tried painting, was not contented with it; went into the army, was dissatisfied with it, and so came back to his first love again, the violin, and went to it. When he first made up his mind to that, he returned to solitude for eight solid weeks and did nothing except practice finger exercises, and from then till now he has daily gone through a narrow gate and down a straitened way of discipline. But it has been worth it.

What are the prerequisites of greatness in any realm? All of them, in Jesus' sense of the word, are narrow. *Attention* is narrow. When Gladstone was asked the secret of his success he replied in one word, "Concentration." The worthwhile mind can focus, but the inattentive mind sprawls every which way. *Decisiveness* is narrow. We cannot decide vaguely and in general; we must decide in particular. The decisive mind defines, excludes, wills this and not that, but the indecisive mind is a vagabond on a broad road. *Loyalty* is narrow. It binds me to a definite devotion. When I love my friend I am not loosely free; I do not wish to be loosely free; my limitation is my glory; I love my friend. But the unloyal man travels a broad road; he has no attachments; he is devoted to no friend; he is a man without a country—broad is the gate and wide is the way.

Here, as so often, Jesus is not so much a painter of beautiful ideals as a proclaimer of universal laws. Nothing left loose ever does anything creative. No horse gets anywhere until he is harnessed. No steam or gas ever drives anything until it is confined. No Niagara is ever turned into light and power until it is tunneled. No life ever grows great until it is focused, dedicated, disciplined.

One of the widest gaps in human experience is the gap between what we say we want to be and our willingness to discipline ourselves to get there. From the homeliest aspects of life—people who say they want to reduce ten pounds, but who will not discipline themselves to do it— to the greatest aspects of life—people who say they want to be Christians, but who will not leave their meandering course of inattentive, indecisive, undevoted living to achieve it—how wide the chasm is between our professed ideals and our willingness to pay the cost! And the cost in every realm is always self-discipline.

Today we confront a world that presses this matter home. One nation has shaken the earth to its foundations, and at the source of its power to do that one hears that nation's leaders commanding the people, Give up butter for guns. We all pray that such discipline may not be necessary here, but it is preposterous to suppose that we in America can preserve our democracy by living in a fool's paradise, with loose morals, disintegrated family life, self-interest taking precedence over public welfare, and a general attitude of loose and easygoing living. Broad is that gate and wide is that way, but it leadeth to destruction. And the very pith and marrow of the matter are here: Nothing worth having in this world, least of all democracy, can be achieved save as the cost of it is paid in self-discipline.

Nevertheless, a second mood within us rises in protest against this truth: I resent restraint and repression, it says; I want to do what I please, follow my whims, fancies, and passions; I want to let myself go. To which the answer seems plain to anyone who knows modern psychology at all. Which self do you want to let go? Do not tell us that you have only one self! You have a lot of selves. No one escapes the elemental problem that James M. Barrie's character, Sentimental Tommy, so well describes when he struggles to make up his mind: "It's easy to you that has just one mind, but if you had as many minds as I have—!" Self-discipline, therefore, begins of necessity at home within our own lives. Not all our selves can have gangway, or if we try to give it to them our inner life will be a mess that

216

even the psychiatrists cannot put to rights. Some chosen self, out of all these many selves, must assume the regency within, must arrange the hierarchy of our loves and interests, establishing some government in the soul so that what we wish on top shall be on top and what we wish subdued shall be obedient. Self-dedication is a basic psychological necessity.

In the chapel at Harvard University is a tablet in memory of old Dr. Peabody, and the end of the inscription runs thus:

His Precept was Glorified by His Example
    While for Thirty-Three Years
He moved among the Teachers and Students of Harvard
    College
And Wist not that His Face Shone.

Facing that kind of life, what does one mean by letting oneself go? Such a man as that inscription celebrates, among all the selves that thronged his life, chose which self should lead, and which should follow after. Unless one's life within is to be a mere mob, it must, one way or another, be organized, integrated, made into hierarchy with supreme values ascendant. All modern psychology at its best underlines the ancient saying: "He that ruleth his spirit is better than he that taketh a city."

It is a strange thing that so many people should talk of doing what they please in a world where modern science has come. No scientist in his special realm thinks he can do what he pleases. Tackle any new problem in the laboratory, strive after any new discovery, and there are countless ways of missing the mark, finding nothing, coming out nowhere.

Broad is the gate and wide the way that leads to no discovery. But only one way leads to that particular truth you seek; there is only one way of so fulfilling the law-abiding conditions that you will get what you are after. Narrow is that gate.

I do not know why God so made the world that the wrong way is broad and the right way is narrow, but this is the way he made it, and in view of that I stand in fear of a sentimental kind of religion which forgets that. It was when Ophelia went crazy that she began distributing flowers indiscriminately to everybody. Some persons want a religion like that, and come to church, I fear, hoping that the preacher will imitate Ophelia and promiscuously distribute sweet messages—"Pansies, that's for thoughts." Jesus was not at all like that. Go through his teaching and his life from beginning to end and see if you can find anything sentimental; lovely, yes! beautiful, yes! but through it all a realistic facing of facts and a realistic statement of universal spiritual laws. There are as many ways of messing life up as there are ways of missing truth in a scientific laboratory, but if we wish a life not messed up, then there is only one way and the gate is narrow—dedication, interior organization, integration, discipline, self-control.

Recall that great phrase of Ignatius Loyola about the man who puts on spurs, but no bridle, to ride a fiery horse. Too many of us have been doing that with ourselves in this country—spurs, but no bridle, to ride a fiery horse— and now we face a world where a dilemma confronts us. Either we are going to discipline ourselves for our own sake, the nation's sake, and the world's, or else discipline will be imposed on us from without.

Nevertheless, still another mood, native to us all, rises in protest against this truth. I hate coercion, it says; I resent repression; I want to be my own master and not the slave of the codes and prescriptions of society; I want to be free.

That is what Jesus wanted. "Ye shall know the truth, and the truth shall make you free." Throughout the New Testament the note of freedom everywhere resounds: "Where the Spirit of the Lord is, there is liberty." Moreover, at the center of Jesus' ministry and of Paul's Epistles is a revolt against the small, enslaving scrupulosities of the ancient legal codes. Ask the Pharisees about Jesus, and they would have said that he himself was a rebel, refusing obedience to the prescriptions of the law, and traveling a dangerously broad road in a perilously loose and undisciplined manner. A friend of mind on a train trip sat behind a mother and her small son. She began saying "Don't" as soon as she came in, and my friend counted. Fifty-nine times in one hour and a half she said "Don't" to that boy. No one wants to live under such restriction, and least of all is Jesus' ethic like that.

At the start, therefore, we may expect his sympathy when we protest against repression and want freedom. Not all our so-called American looseness has been bad. Many trivial scrupulosities have masqueraded under the disguise of discipline. A woman of my generation can remember the Dean of Vassar College saying to the students: "Young ladies, I hope that I may never see the day when you will so far forget your dignity and delicacy as to appear upon the campus without gloves." All the way from that to endless rules and regulations in the moral realm, caricatures of discipline have cluttered up the field. No man is worth his salt who does not sometimes rise in rebellion, smash through some nonsensical repression, and claim his freedom.

When, however, we are through with that, we still face an inescapable fact—there are some things we can never be free from. Free thinking is not freedom from the laws of thought. Free living is not freedom from the laws of life. All scientific creativity goes back to obedience to scientific law. All artistic creativeness depends upon obedience to the laws of beauty. No one is free until he is mastered.

> Make me a captive, Lord,
> And then I shall be free;
> Force me to render up my sword,
> And I shall conq'ror be.

That is not poetry alone, but basic psychological fact.

Mark Twain, for example, lost his fortune. The accumulations of his brilliant life work tumbled into an abyss of debt. According to the public law he could have escaped all responsibility in bankruptcy. Why did he not travel that broad and easy way? Why did he voluntarily assume the burden of those debts, circumnavigating the globe, even, although on the threshold of old age, tirelessly speaking and writing until he paid the last penny? He told us why in one brief sentence: "Honor is a harder master than the law." Something inside himself he had to live up to. In Tennyson's phrase, he was "loyal to the royal" in himself. Narrow was that gate, and straitened that way, but it led to life. That kind of disciplined character is not a matter of small scrupulosities.

Today we may well celebrate the men and women in high or humble places who thus have within themselves something fine that they must live up to. They are the prerequisite of democracy. The storms of life beat on them, as they beat on all of us today, but they have a compass, something within them that they are true to and steer by. Over against that kind of life put the loose, lax, immoralism of our generation, where many voices have cried, like the witches in *Macbeth,* "Fair is foul, and foul is fair." We preachers are tempted to think of such loose living solely in ethical terms. We call it sin. But it is more than that. It is psychological and emotional disintegration. Such a life never gets itself together around any center, never is dedicated and disciplined to any end. Such a man has to say, like a character in one of H. G. Wells' novels, "I'm not a man but a mob." Only one who has been mastered by something worth being mastered by ever can be a real person.

Wherever you find a real person in any realm, Toscanini in music, for example, one thing is present—a devotion that it is his pride, joy, and freedom to live up to and discipline himself for. That is different from letting yourself go. That is not the same thing as subservience to conventional codes. That is having something within you, stimulating, empowering, controlling, around which your life grows integral and unified, so that your joy and liberation are in living up to it and out from it.

Until religion means that to a man it is an ineffective conventionality. When in Shakespeare's drama the Earl of Kent went out to King Lear in his exile to offer his allegiance, he gave this as his explanation: "You have that in your countenance which I would fain call master." When a man says that to Christ in earnest, until within himself

Christ's spirit and way of life become an organizing center, an inner criterion, then he is a Christian.

America today desperately needs people who thus within themselves have something that they must live up to. See how we sit in comfort here! Destitution will not mark our dinner tables when we go home; fear will not haunt our night with sirens warning us that the bombing planes are coming. What right have we to this ease? I am not saying, Give up butter for guns. May that kind of coercion be spared us! But in a day when all the world on both sides of the battle line—often with a courage and self-sacrifice that make us salute the grandeur of human nature even while we are appalled at what human nature does— is displaying magnificent self-dedication and self-control, by what exemption have we a right to live a lax, loose, unbuttoned life?

If America should ever fail, if after the promise of its start, and the unexampled marvel of its opportunity, it should come from a fair springtime to a barren autumn, what would be the reason? Not lack of laws, not lack of outward regulation, not lack of dictatorship even, for we would try that before we fell, but lack of people who so disciplined themselves from within that they were self-propelled, having liberty because they deserved it, keeping democracy because they helped create it, running themselves so well from the inside that they did not need to be run from the outside. And that profound and inner matter is, at its deepest, a great religion's gift. For the roots of a self-disciplined character are profoundly spiritual—faith that there are values worth being dedicated to, faith that there are ends worth being self-disciplined for, faith that beyond the torture of these years, by God's grace, there is a possible world, decent, fraternal, peaceable, that self-disciplined men and nations can build. When such faith is lost, it is all up with democracy. And the place for this kind of living to begin is within each of us. Whatever else we can or cannot do for the world, at least we can give it one more life that proves Tennyson's words true:

> Self-reverence, self-knowledge, self-control,
> These three alone lead life to sovereign power.

❋

The Place of Self-Discipline *

JAMES REID

Strive to enter in at the strait gate: for many, I say unto you, will seek to enter in, and shall not be able.—Luke 13:24

Enter ye in at the strait gate: for wide is the gate and broad is the way, that leadeth to destruction . . . because strait is the gate, and narrow is the way, which leadeth unto life.

—Matthew 7:13, 14

If any man will come after me, let him deny himself, and take up his cross, and follow me.

—Matthew 16:24

*From *Facing Life with Christ* by James Reid. Copyright 1940 by Whitmore and Smith (Abingdon Press). Used by permission.

Wherefore if thy hand or thy foot offend thee, cut them off, and cast them from thee: it is better for thee to enter into life halt or maimed, rather than, having two hands or two feet, to be cast into everlasting fire.—Matthew 18:8

Whosoever will save his life shall lose it: and whosoever will lose his life for my sake shall find it.—Matthew 16:25

IT IS IMPOSSIBLE to face life in the Christian way without coming upon the demand for what Jesus calls self-denial. It is true that, from the deepest point of view, the Christian life is a growth from within. It is a life which proceeds from a new spirit born in us as the spontaneous response to the love of God, in which his purpose takes possession of us and our will becomes one with his. The Christian life is thus lifted out of the sphere of mere obedience to rules or regulations into the realm of love, in which conduct is directed by insight into the will of God, and finds its motive power in love to him.

But this level is not easily or immediately reached. The old primitive self has had a long start in most cases. Habits of self-will have been formed. Pride of loveless ambition or even crude passion have twined their roots around the soul, choking its life. Though we seek to make God's purpose ours, that purpose must win its full control in many a struggle with the insurgent egotism. We find it hard to take our hands off the management of our own life or to prevent our own lower purposes and self-seeking desires from usurping God's place. When Christ comes in, as old John Owen said, "He hath no easy landing-place." There is a struggle for possession, in which the strong man who has been in charge must be bound, as Jesus said. Time after time there are decisions to be made in which the old self must be dethroned so that the new self in fellowship with God may be free.

The conflict may come in various forms. It may come through the imperious demands of the instincts and appetites, claiming their satisfaction in the physical functions of hunger and sex. It may come in the love of power over others, or in some way to use them as means to our ends. It may come when the selfish claim for comfort or pre-eminence is met by the demand for love or the call to some unselfish service. In all these ways the pull of the old life, rooted in habit and sustained by the emotional forces of instinct and imagination, is brought face to face with a narrow way which in our hearts we know to be the way of Christ.

Facing this conflict, we are met by some sayings of Christ which sound hard and forbidding. "If any man will come after me, let him deny himself and take up his cross and follow me." That is forbidding enough. But there is an even more stringent note. "If thy right hand offend thee, cut it off and cast it from thee. It is better for a man to enter into life maimed than having two hands and two feet to be cast into hell fire." This stern demand for self-discipline runs through the message of Jesus with a penetrating and challenging note. It is a demand for renunciation, for the surrender, at various points, of comfort and ease and physical and personal satisfactions.

This demand for renunciation has been strongly repudiated from various quarters. It inspired the familiar stanza of Swinburne:

Thou hast conquered, O pale Galilean.
The world has grown grey with thy breath.

It has been attacked by the modern psychology that insists on the individual's right of self-expression and for the satisfaction of instinct as a means to that end. They forget, of course, that if this claim to the right of self-expression were to be admitted without a clear understanding of what self it is we are to express, it would justify the thief and coward as well as the libertine, for the instincts of fear and acquisitiveness have equal rights to be expressed. Jesus was all for the right of self-expression. "I am come," he said "that they might have life and that they might have it to the full." A Christian is a man who has for the first time become himself. He experiences, in surrender to God's purpose, a release of capacities that have been held in bondage. It was in order that we might win this freedom that Christ's demand for self-denial was made. The vital difference between Christ's point of view and that of others is in the nature of the self that is to find its freedom.

The demand for self-denial has been in many cases resented because it has been wrongly interpreted. It has been represented as the demand for asceticism—the cult that makes physical hardship and the suppression of all physical appetite an end in itself. The hair shirt and the other methods of self-inflicted pain are extreme examples. The lives of the saints tell the story of many good people who made asceticism their ideal of life and claimed for it the authority of Jesus. But Jesus was no ascetic in this sense of the word. No one could spend so much time healing crippled bodies, and have the contempt for the body which lies behind the ascetic outlook on life. He admired the birds with their perfection of physical beauty, and no less surely must his mind have seen in the healthy frame the craftsmanship of God. In all maltreatment of the body by disease or by the cruelty of men he saw the work of devils. He would have had nothing but pity for self-inflicted pain. He enjoyed good food, though he was never a slave to it and put it in a very secondary place, as we gather from his gentle rebuke of Martha's fussy anxiety to provide elaborate hospitality. He was charged by his enemies with being a "gluttonous man and a wine-bibber." This is a slander, of course, but it proves that when he was invited to a dinner with his friends, he felt no difficulty about sharing their food and drink. The root of asceticism is that it regards the body and its satisfactions as evil, and exalts self-denial into a virtue. There may be in it more than a trace of the subtle pleasure of self-martyrdom. But in any case, at the center of it there is often a form of pride that destroys any claim it may have to be a virtue.

What was it that lay behind the call of Christ for self-denial? It was not as an end in itself or as a virtue that he demanded it, but as a means to our liberation, our freedom to seek God's purpose. Self-discipline is for self-dedication. It is a means to the true fulfillment of life. We can see this clearly when we are called to refuse or suppress some insurgent instinct such as the instinct of sex. Jesus was not married, but that does not imply any ascetic attitude to sex such as we find in the teaching of St. Paul. His love for children, his genial interest in the home, his reverence for women and motherhood, and his use of parental love as a mirror of the love of God, all reveal a sound and healthy valuation of the love which has its physical roots in sex. If a home of his own was ruled out of his scheme of life, it was because his love for all men and women demanded an expression in service which put marriage out of the question for him. "There be some," he said, "who are eunuchs for the sake of the Kingdom of God." His principle for the right satisfaction of every instinct is clear. It is that this satisfaction must be related to the purpose of life, which means God's purpose in us and for us. All satisfaction out of relation with the total purpose of life is of the nature of sin. It means that self is at that point in control. The result of such self-satisfaction can only be bondage and futility. This was the verdict of the poet Burns. He found that pleasure can never be an end in itself or it is lost in the moment of attaining it.

Pleasures are like poppies spread,
You seize the flower; its bloom is shed.

Happiness of any kind can only be the accompaniment of activities which are directed to the true purpose of life. It is missed or corrupted unless it comes as the by-product of some higher activity.

If we are seeking God's purpose and not our own satisfaction, some denial of the instincts will be inevitable. They will need to be controlled and may even need to be suppressed. But that will not end in the frustration of life, but in its fulfillment. For the suppressed instinct will find its liberation along other channels. The well-known principle of sublimation comes into play. The instinct which is denied, for the moment, its immediate satisfaction will yield up its force in the increased mental and spiritual vigor of life. A rose tree is pruned in the spring. The process may be drastic and might appear to the onlooker to be

228

fatal to the life of the plant. But the sap in the roots and stem finds, through the apparent mutilation, channels for flowering into richer beauty.

This is the process that takes place when some denial of self is made in the interests of the service of others. Many have found fruitful expression and satisfaction for their own starved instincts in the care of little children or in some form of human service. If we are seeking to follow Christ in his service of others, and so to find escape from our imprisoning selves, we will need to deny ourselves. Time will have to be given up. Mental effort that might be spent on the culture of our own lives will be used up in thought for and sympathy with others. Money will have to be spent for others that would otherwise be kept for ourselves. We cannot have it both ways. "Whosoever will save his life shall lose it." If our true life in God's purpose is one which makes the interest of others our own, self must be put on one side. In time this will become a joy. It will be found to be the way of our true freedom. But this will not happen without pain. Such loving service will always have on it the marks of the Cross. Sometimes the choice will appear to involve what amounts to mutilation.

A lady who died not long ago started her career as an artist. She showed such promise that one sound critic declared that if she persevered she might become another Holman Hunt. But when God's purpose became clear to her, it seemed right that she should go to the mission field. It was a desperately hard choice, for it meant the apparent frustration of what seemed to be a genuine gift of God. It was indeed like cutting off a hand or plucking out an eye. But she realized that what God's purpose demanded of her was, as she put it, "to bind her life to the horns of the altar and let God do with it what he willed." In that spirit of surrender she calmly sought the way. It led her to Africa, where she found that her art was of considerable service in her missionary work.

What Christ would have us realize is the true meaning of self-denial. Part of its purpose is concentration. It is like the work of the engineers who take the waters of a river that have been spreading themselves here and there over a wide plain, and confine them in a narrower channel. This is not really cramping their freedom; it is conserving their power. If the purpose of our life is to be fulfilled through the life of God's Spirit in us, there must be concentration. No one has achieved either character or unselfishness unless his life is a co-ordinated unity. He must learn to say with St. Paul, "One thing I do"; and this also, "One thing I am." But concentration can only be achieved at the cost of self-discipline.

The other thing which Christ would have us realize is that self-denial is the secret of liberty, and this is its true purpose. In a book written by an American psychologist in which he describes his spiritual experience, he tells how he awoke to realize the value of Christianity from his own use of Christ's precepts in helping his patients back to normal mental health. He then decided that he must recover the habit of worship. His first decision to return to church was made because he found himself unwilling to go. He went, he says, because he did not want to go. He realized that his unwillingness to go to church was restricting his liberty of action. It had therefore to be broken down by a deliberate act of self-discipline, if that liberty was to be regained.

This may seem a strange way to put it, but there is

truth behind it. Every habit that self-will or self-indulgence forms is a restriction of liberty. Every prejudice against a certain line of conduct, unless it be against something which we know is wrong, is a fence that restricts our freedom. It may also reveal to us some capacity which needs to be developed. We can discover a good deal about ourselves by the investigation of the things we do not like doing. The fact that a person is unwilling to make friends shows in that very fact the greater need to exercise the friendly spirit. If we find ourselves unwilling to pray or incapable of worship, it only shows the greater need for developing these capacities; for the mark of spiritual decay is that we lose the spiritual hunger. The first step in its recovery may be as painful and costly as the first use of a limb that has been out of action for some time, but there is only one thing to be done. These fences must be broken down, and they can only be broken down by the deliberate practice of self-denial at that point, by doing, in fact, the things that we do not like to do.

Professor William James says that he made it the habit of his life to do one act of deliberate self-denial every day, in order to keep his will in training. This is the true asceticism, and it is of the same value for the spirit as athletics is for the body. It preserves our freedom to obey the call of the spirit, to be ready and able, unhindered, to seek God's purpose in our life whatever it be. Freedom is not a gift that is ours by nature. It is a prize that has to be won. It is for the achievement of our true freedom that we are here. For our true freedom is not our liberty to do as we like. It is our power to become and to do what we ought. And our fullest freedom, as St. Paul said, is only found and realized when love becomes the master motive and guiding principle of our life. Then, and only then, are we fully ourselves.

It is for the achievement of this freedom that Christ calls us to deny ourselves, not because self-denial is a virtue or has any merit in itself. Christ was ready to suffer pain and to impose it on himself, but he never glorified it as having any intrinsic beauty of its own. The strange beauty that shines from the Cross and makes him more lovely in his broken body than any Apollo, comes from the quality of perfect love that could turn these ugly wounds into the emblems of victory, because they found their place in that abandonment of self to God's loving purpose for the world. There is a phrase that has puzzled and startled many people in his words about self-denial. It is that which speaks of "taking up the Cross." This picture he is calling up is that of a man on the road to crucifixion, carrying his cross as those who were about to be executed were forced to do. It seems a cruel picture to ask us to put into our plan of life, even into the purpose of God for us. There are some who have literally had to do it, going to the very stake for the sake of the Kingdom of God. But that cannot be God's deliberate purpose for us. Nor should we try to fit our self-denials, however hard, into that picture and speak of them as "carrying a Cross." The explanation of Christ's words is to be found in this thought of achieving our freedom. The man who carried his cross to the place of execution was already dead to the world. The old life was over for him. The clamorous appeals of egotism had lost their power. He belonged already to another world. That is the kind of freedom Christ would have us seek and find—the detachment from the appeals and the imperious impulses of self-centered desires. He bids us claim and win our freedom to see God's purpose and to live in his rule. That rule, in the measure of its complete possession of our wills, is the secret of our freedom. But that freedom can be won, to begin with, only by deliberate self-denial.

The same thing is true if the love of others, by which we seek God's purpose in them, is to come fully and deeply into our life. It is true that love sets us free from self. It comes in to fill the house and drive self out. The Aggressive Lover must win his own way. We cannot achieve this love to others by any effort of our own. But it is also true that before this love which Christ awakens can fully invade our life, we must often deal self a blow that will loosen its grip. The idol must sometimes be torn from the throne before God can take his place there. As in the body, adhesions must sometimes be broken down by a surgical operation before the new life can flow freely in our veins. The conflict may center in some particular pleasure or habit—the taproot of self which at that point only can be overcome.

In Bunyan's dream the Pilgrim saw a palace, and before the door of it a great company assembled, hestitating to go in because the door was held by armed men. Then he saw one step out of the group and say to the man who was taking the names of the would-be entrants, "Set down my name, sir"; and drawing his sword, he prepared for battle. The Kingdom of God may need to be entered by us with a drawn sword, for the armed men will be the various forms of self. In that encounter we may even be maimed, as it were, but we shall be entering into life.

From Helped to Helper

❧ ❧ ❧

There are some people in our congregations who need to be challenged more than they need to be counseled. Some need a vision of something to achieve more than they need therapy. Some will never realize their full potential until they are challenged by a task that demands their best. Some will never find self-fulfillment by looking within; they need to forget themselves in the interest of others, to give themselves to a cause greater than they are. It is those that lose themselves who find themselves.

There are some causes, including service to the church, that are being crippled and limited because there are not enough people who have a sense of personal responsibility and a vision of service that causes them to dedicate their time, their strength, and their ability to Christian service.

As a minister views his congregation, he sees many people who could be making a much greater contribution than they are, whose lives could be enriched if they had a greater desire to serve. This was a constant emphasis in Jesus' preaching. Over and over again he demanded a life of service. For him this was the mark of true greatness. "Whoever would be great among you must be your servant, and whoever would be first among you must be slave of all" (Mark 10:43-44). Since Jesus placed such a predominant emphasis on service in his preaching, pastors today should also treat it with due concern.

It is also a matter for pastoral counseling. Many may not serve or may avoid responsibility because of feelings of inadequacy or fear of failure. Urging them on is not enough without first freeing them from the feelings that prevent service. Others have attempted to serve only to be frustrated and discouraged. This also is a personal matter and can best be handled on a counseling basis. When the pastor does this, he not only strengthens an individual but also advances a cause.

Service is an individual matter. Not all can serve in the same way. In vocational counseling we have learned that people have different talents and abilities, different interests, likes, and dislikes. Only as we understand the individual and the vocation under consideration can we help him make a vocational choice that is mature and realistic. The same principles apply here. Some counseling on service will include service through one's vocation; some will involve service through the program of the church or other needed causes. Always individual capabilities, interests, and backgrounds should be considered.

The challenge to service, the biblical demands for service, and the opportunities for service can be stressed from the pulpit.

(1) Through preaching a pastor can present the biblical imperative of a life of service. One can accept or reject the teachings of Jesus as he wishes. But he cannot accept them without accepting such a life as one of his primary demands. "If any man would come after me, let him deny himself and take up his cross and follow me" (Matt. 16:24).

(2) Through preaching a pastor can motivate and inspire people to grow out of their self-centeredness and into a life of self-forgetfulness. History and biography are filled with inspirational illustrations of how this has been done.

(3) Through preaching a pastor can make the people aware of the fact that we are all indebted to others, both in the past and in the present, who have lived lives of self-forgetful, often sacrificial service. Our only adequate response is to attempt to render some service in return.

235

(4) Through preaching a pastor can warn of the sin of uselessness. The priest and Levite in the story of the good Samaritan were condemned not because they did wrong but because they did nothing. In chapter 25 of Matthew it reads, "As you did it not to one of the least of these, you did it not to me" (verse 45).

(5) Through preaching a pastor can surround all forms of service with dignity and meaning. The value Jesus placed on obscure service is amazing. Even the giving of a cup of cold water was an act of value in the sight of God. Thus Jesus placed the ability to serve within the reach of all. It is not something limited to the brilliant, to those in high office. Every member of the congregation can be of service.

(6) Through preaching the pastor can make people aware that service to God means service to men. "As you did it to one of the least of these my brethren, you did it to me" (Matt. 25:40). Opportunities for service are always available. As John Watson said, "Be kind, every one you meet is fighting a hard battle."

(7) Through preaching the pastor can present a realistic picture of the nature of service. It is not easy to serve. It makes great demands. At times it is discouraging and frustrating, but it is rewarding. Even Paul experienced this. He wrote, "And let us not grow weary in well-doing, for in due season we shall reap, if we do not lose heart" (Gal. 6:9).

(8) Through preaching the pastor can lead people to life's highest sense of self-fulfillment. In challenging people to lives of service he is not only advancing a cause, he is helping the persons who serve. The servants of humanity have found an inner satisfaction which the pleasure-seekers cannot know.

(9) Through preaching the pastor can provide reassurance that there are sources of strength which come to those who give of themselves in trust and dedication. Clara Barton once said, "You must never think of anything except the need

236

Christianity has, from the beginning, been exhibiting the world's principles reversed as in a looking-glass. When the disciples were accused of turning the world upside down, there was more truth in the charge than was at first supposed; and as in the case of the text, more truth than their accusers ever thought of putting there. The Gospel turns things about in a very astonishing way. It teaches that the humblest are the most exalted, the weakest are the strongest, the poorest are the richest, the sorrowful are the happiest; and those who lose their life are those who save it.

A recent novelist has founded a popular story on this principle of reversal; he has given us a world in which the poor rule and the rich serve, and in which he is the happiest man who is so fortunate as to find some one who is willing to receive a favor from him. Mr. Bellamy's "Looking Backward" is but a setting forth of these reversed principles. Society says, "Every man for himself. Might is right. Let the strongest survive." Mr. Bellamy says society is wrong. Its root is selfishness, its fruit an apple of Sodom. True society must spring from a different principle. Every man shall love his neighbor as himself; right is might. The weakest shall have an equal chance with the strongest.

Such statements as these are pronounced visionary and Utopian by those who assume to be the practical conservators of our socials; even the Christian community finds it hard to believe in its own Gospel of an unselfish society, wherein dwelleth righteousness, and it is about as hard in its criticisms upon the writers who propose to bring the millennium about in a practical way as is the veriest unbeliever. Selfishness is the original sin. It is the tap-root of all the evil that has afflicted the race. The philosopher of the selfish school, who shows that all society is but the efflorescence and fruit of this selfish spirit, gives us the best account of things as they are. Only the philosopher of the Christian school can give us any account of the things as they ought to be and will be. The mission of the Nazarene was to lay His hands upon the throttle-valve of society and reverse its disastrous on-rush to destruction. His life from Bethlehem to Calvary was a series of surprises to those who were looking for the Messiah. They were looking for a king in gold and glory; He came a servant and a daily laborer. They looked for self-assertion; He came in self-denial. They looked for a crown; He brought a cross.

I have studied this subject of our Lord's sacrifice much. I have tried to absorb its truth into my own personality, so as to be able to present it in my preaching as a reality rather than a theory. Too much of theory I fear we have had in our pulpits during the past century; too much talk about the atonement, and not enough of the spirit of it. There is danger of theorizing the whole question over into the realm of the unreal, and of so overstating it as to rob it of its practical worth. Self-denial, for example, is sometimes made to mean the complete surrender of one's personality, or rather the extinction of it through some process of penance or self-inflicted hardship. I do not believe in the sentiment of that hymn:

Oh, to be nothing, nothing,
    Only to lie at his feet,
A broken and emptied vessel
    For the Saviour's use made meet.

The Lord forbid that we should be whining, canting nothings and nobodies, and preserve us from being broken and emptied pitchers in His service. I want to be something, though it be a small thing; I want to have a whole full personality, a self endowed with all the powers of selfhood, to present to Christ. An earthen jar it may be, and filled with earthly water, but whole and full to the brim, that the Christ of Cana may transmute them into the wine that is of His kingdom. A true self-love and self-respect are to be commended. A lack of these qualities leads a man to neglect health and influence, and to become a mere cipher in God's great aggregate of the world's saving forces. You must take care of yourself if you would be fitted to take care of others. There are times when suicidal neglect of sleep and diet and recreation are justifiable—time when to save life you must risk life—but these times are not common.

Self-sacrifice is nothing as an end in and of itself. The man who sits on a pedestal with Simon Stylites under the delusion that there is any virtue in letting his finger nails grow through the palm of his clenched hand is making a fatal mistake. And yet this is the kind of a mistake that a good part of Christendom has been laboring under. It has gone on long pilgrimages, and shut itself up in dark cells, and tortured the poor body until the soul was glad to leave it, thinking it was winning heaven, while all the time it was in mistaken ignorance of the true spirit of denial, which has for its end not the mortification of the physical self, but the happiness and the good of some one not the self.

Do you want to know whether you are a Christian or not? Well, you can tell very easily. Just imagine the Christ

240

of the Gospels sitting here today. Watch him. Here come a number of curiosity-seekers who want to hear what He has to say of Himself and His cause; but He is tired; He has been working all day. Will He give up His personal comfort for the sake of teaching these indifferent people? Would you do it? Here comes a Magdalen with downcast and tearful eyes, more sinned against than sinning, yet she esteems herself the chief of sinners, and wonders if sin like hers can be forgiven. Will the sinless Master even look at her, or think of recognizing her? Would you? Over there in the corner, with his face half hidden, penitent and troubled, sits Peter. He has three times denied his Lord. He has turned his back on Him. Will the Lord notice him? Will He forgive him? Would you?

Out in the street yonder, down in the alley, and up in the attic tenements, are scores of sinners who care no more for the Lord and His house then they do for Athena and her temple. Many are lame in purpose, halt in all kinds of spiritual activity, blind to the truth. Will the Lord of the feast go out and compel them to come in? Will He suffer much that He may save them? Would you? Would you feed the hungry, clothe the naked, visit the prisoner, and minister unto the sick? In a word, would you spend your heart's best love, your heart's best life, in unselfish ministrations as Christ did? If you would, you are a Christian. If you would not, whatever your profession, whatever your knowledge of the Scriptures, whatever your adherence to the outward forms of religion, you have no right to that name. I am not a pessimist, nor am I an alarmist; I do not believe in too much fault-finding; but I am more and more impressed with the conviction that the trouble with the

241

church today is not due, as some aver, to laxity in doctrine, but to a prevalence of selfishness.

I happened to be coming through Bangor a few weeks ago on the last day of an agricultural fair. The cars were crowded with all sorts of country folks who had come into the city for their annual recreation and sight-seeing. A grand chance to study human nature at its best and at its worst. Such a scramble for seats as the train backed into the station to be filled. Everybody wanted the best seat. Great burly men, with the strength of their shameless manhood, ruthlessly crowded from the platform delicate women with babes in their arms. One man rushed in and preempted two double seats, turning over the back of one, fencing off his claim with an umbrella, which he held stoutly across the entrance. One woman took defiant possession of two seats with bag and baggage, and successfully held the spare one by telling all applicants that it was engaged. And then what solid comfort they all seemed to take in seeing the great crowd of late-comers anxiously scurrying through the aisles in a vain search for a resting place. How glad these fortunate ones were in their plush comfort, that they had denied themselves a last look at the fine horses and the fair grounds, and by that act of self-denial had succeeded in getting into the train ahead of their neighbors. And yet the majority of these people were good, respectable people of the good state of Maine. Many of them would doubtless suffer much to bless a brother man in need. Many of them were Christians, I presume. They were simply yielding to those selfish impulses, which are the surest indications that the world is, as yet, far from the standard of Him who pleased not Himself.

Such impulses are working in the Church of Christ

today, unconsciously, but yet tending to the same exclusive results as those witnessed on that train of cars. The church itself is in danger of becoming a special train on board of which the Christians are more exercised concerning their own comfort and destination than they are concerning the destination and comfort of the surging crowd outside. These things ought not to be. We see our weaknesses. We know that we are naturally selfish; that we often consider our personal comfort before the spiritual and temporal welfare of those about us, and yet there are times when we rise to the higher vantage ground of our faith; when a noble resolve moves us to do and to suffer for the salvation of men and the betterment of the world. Oh, how mean and insignificant our selfish selves seem as we stand at these lookout stations of our experience! We try to see ourselves as others see us; as the angels see us.

I was standing on Mt. Kineo a few weeks ago,—a magnificent mass of solid hornblend, raising 1,100 feet from the bosom of the lake, one side a perpendicular wall capped with beetling cliffs, which seemed ever ready to plunge into the inky waters that lie crumpled and trembling in a sort of Dantean gloom at their base. From the top of the wall I looked down upon the lake and curving shore. Boats like tiny eggshells with their mites of humanity floated here and there within the range of my vision. Men and women that looked like pigmies moved about on the land. The sensation was a strange one. The world seemed so large and the men so small. I could not help exclaiming, "What is man that thou art mindful of him?" It takes but an altitude of half a mile to reduce him to the proportions of an ant; what must he seem from the altitude of heaven? An insect that lives his little day, that buzzes and circles over his bit of marsh, or fen, or glade; that struggles over his little mound of earth, collects his pile of glittering sand, and then lies down beside it to die, and be forgotten by a world that hardly knew he ever lived.

Ah, no, not this, I said, not this, except he be that smallest of the Creator's works, a supremely selfish man! If such he be, living within self, and for self, loveless and Christless, always getting and never giving, he shall at last lie down beside his gettings, and the lowly pile shall mark the stature of his manhood; but if the spirit of Christ be his, if his personality be charged with the electric potency of love, he shall make for himself a place in God's world, the altitude of which shall not be measured by Ossa piled upon Kineo, and Pelion upon Ossa. For when you are able to comprehend the breadth and length and height of the love of Christ, which passeth knowledge, you shall know the stature of that manhood or womanhood which is filled and moved by that love. Measure yourself, my brother, by the Cross today.

✻

Bear Ye One Another's Burdens *

HAROLD W. KASER

I VENTURE TO BEGIN this sermon in a rather unusual place: the attic of a church. Most people have never visited a church attic. Few of them are as intricate or as interesting

*Reprinted by permission from the July-August 1962 issue of *Pulpit Digest;* copyright 1962 by The Pulpit Digest Publishing Company. Also by permission of the author.

244

as the one where the Hunchback of Notre Dame lived, yet some of them have an intriguing story to tell. Such was the case of a church in Michigan a few years ago, for in its attic a Chinese student had lived for four years. Before living in this church attic, he had attended Michigan University. There, in his new surroundings, he found that life was too much for him. He failed in his courses and thought that this would mean disgrace for his parents who lived in China. So he hid away in this church attic, unknown to all the world.

At night he would go down to the church kitchen and eat what was left over from church suppers. His clothing he picked out of the rummage bags that were left after rummage sales. He was terribly lonely. Sundays were special days for him, for he would crawl down behind the choir loft where he could be as close to the choir members as possible. The only thing that separated him from the choir members was a thin wall. O, how he longed to reach out and touch the people. Then one day he was discovered. When his story became known, it was spread over all the newspapers in the country, but, best of all, the congregation of that church took him in. Now he no longer lived in the attic of this church, a lonely person, unknown to all, but he became part of their fellowship.

At that point that congregation became the redeeming community spoken of so often in the pages of the New Testament.

At that point that congregation became the loving fellowship of God which knows no barrier of race or color or social standing.

At that point that congregation exercised the New Testament admonition to rejoice with those who rejoice and to weep with those who weep.

At that point the members of that congregation learned anew the meaning of bearing the burden of another.

Early in the pages of the New Testament the writers speak about Christian community. It began with Jesus and the Twelve. It continued to the seventy apostles, to the early Church in the Book of Acts, to the congregations that were started by Paul all over Asia Minor. An outstanding characteristic of these Christian communities was that the members learned how to bear one another's burdens. They were linked heart and soul together so that they became the redeeming and the redeemed community, the forgiven and the forgiving fellowship. Hence they were called, not only the Church, but also the very body of Christ, and each one a member of that body. They needed each other, how desperately they needed each other. In that body, the hand could not say to the foot, "I have no need of thee," nor could the foot say to the hand, "I have no need of thee." When one part of the body suffers, does not every other part suffer also? And when one part of the body rejoices, does not every part rejoice?

In our day of cliques and class, divisiveness and aloofness, this New Testament principle of bearing one another's burdens is something that could stand more emphasis. Everywhere we go there is the apparent need of bearing one another's burdens. In business, in the community, in the family, and most of all in the church, we have become an exploding population in a lonely crowd.

While there are more people in the world today than ever before, perhaps we are lonelier than at any other point in history. Certainly we have more burdens to bear than ever before. We live in a world where the forces that divide us threaten to destroy us. Nations are divided by rival systems of politics and economics. Groups within nations are divided by class and race consciousness. Communities are divided by different loyalties. Our only hope lies in a force that unites us into a sense of community, where we no longer hold each other at arm's length, but where love enslaves each member of the community to bear the burdens of every other member of the community.

Let's talk about the Church, our church. Like the Chinese student, there are many within the walls of our church who are suffering, who are lonely, who are burdened. They long to reach out in an effort to grasp a helping hand. Fear of rejection often keeps them from really making known the depth of their despair. Days go into months, and months go into years, and years go into a lifetime, and they can sing only too well the Negro spiritual: "Nobody knows the trouble I'se seen."

Nobody knows! That should never have to be said by anybody in the Christian community. The reason it should not have to be said is not because the church can have a professional staff to minister to the people, but because every member of the Christian community is enslaved by love to every other member of the Christian community. In that enslavement they bear one another's burdens and so fulfill the law of Christ.

Many of you still remember about five years ago when this church reached out a helping hand and took one in whose life was a long story of burdens. For forty years he was in and out of the community, not always respectable,

247

but always lonely and troubled. Finally he found in this church a new life. How did it happen? One man in this congregation, now an elder, became a burden bearer for him. Then there were others who shared their concern. Though he lived only six months after we shared his burdens, that testimony of Christian concern will forever be an inspiring memory to all who had a part in it. So grateful was this man's sister, who lives some distance from here, that frequently on the anniversary of his death she sends a letter and a gift of money to add to the memorial fund that was established for him. And who can measure the joy of our Lord at such a time when he sees that we bear one another's burdens?

You see, Christianity is not some vague philosophy you dream about in moments of relaxation. Christianity is a way of life that requires action. When will we learn that the cross of Christ is not a date, 33 A.D., but a timeless fact of history? It is not a piece of wood to which Christ was nailed, it is the way of love that bears the burdens of others. Theologically, Christ bore his cross as a burden of other people. If we are Christ's true followers, there is no way of escaping the burdens of others.

The principle of burden bearing within the Christian community was the basis of our Lord's parable of the Last Judgment in Matthew 25. In that parable Jesus indicated that, when we bear the burden of another, we minister to Christ himself. In the sea of faces gathered around the last judgment each man is singled out in turn. He is asked not about his creed, nor his manner of worship, nor standing in the community. Rather, he is asked what burdens he lifted for the hungry, the thirsty, the stranger, the naked, the sick, and those in prison.

To put this in our language, the questions will be: "What burden did you bear for the poor family on the other side of town?" "Did you ever make any visits to the local jail?" "Did you enter sympathetically into the loneliness of the stranger that moved next door?" And after the question, our Lord will say: "Inasmuch as you did it unto the least of these, my brethren, you did it unto me."

This is why Ernest Crosby wrote the following:

No one could tell me where my soul might be;
I searched for God, and He eluded me;
I sought my brother out, and found all three.

Let's look at the alternative. If we choose not to bear the burdens of others, we are inviting ourselves to end all progress in the Christian community. The Christian community only rises higher as all the members of the Christian community rise together. To leave some with burdens while others try to run ahead is to establish the norm of the community at the level of the burdened. Life then becomes petrified at that level and all growth ceases. When that happens, we can write the Old Testament word, "Ichabod," which means "the glory of the Lord has departed from this place."

No one can read the paper today without becoming aware of the desperate struggle that is going on all over the world for community. People do not take readily to a Robinson Crusoe existence.

There are only two things that bring people into community: a common danger and a common purpose. A common danger drives people together, but a common purpose draws people together.

Right now it looks as though people are being driven together by a common danger. People of one idealogy are driven together out of fear of another idealogy; people of one nation are driven together out of fear of another nation; people of one race are driven together out of fear of another race. Whenever this happens, the community which results never is the type where its members bear one another's burdens. Their only concern is to band together for mutual safety.

Over against this is the concept of Christian community where we are drawn together because we belong together in a common purpose. That purpose is to fulfill the law of Christ. How do we fulfill the law of Christ? Paul said we do this by bearing one another's burdens.

Some of you are sitting beside a neighbor or a member of your family, others are sitting beside a person from the other side of town, and still others are sitting beside strangers. Each of you has burdens, for such is the nature of our life. Some are burdened with loneliness, some by sickness, some by death, some by frustration, some by sin and temptation. Take hope, my friends, for we are in the company of those who are drawn together by love; love that knows no intellectual snobbery, no social superiority, no racial intolerance, no temperamental privilege, no religious bigotry.

The New Testament says that it used to be the custom of similar groups that, as they met and parted, they would greet each other with a holy kiss, the symbol of loving concern. The symbol of concern in our time is the handshake and the spoken word of greeting.

250

May each of you, at the close of this service, greet each other with a handshake of concern, and thereby let each other know that no one in this Christian community need say: "Nobody knows the trouble I'se seen." For then you will know. When you know, you will care. When you care, you will bear the burden of another.

A Note on the Type

The text matter of this book has been set in Intertype Baskerville and the display matter in Times New Roman and Italic.

The original design of Baskerville type dates back to the middle part of the eighteenth century but still remains on the list of elegant designs.

The paper used is Northwest's Bookbinders Text.

Typography is by David Homeier.